MICHAEL FULLAN ✸ CLIF ST. GERMAIN

LEARNING PLACES

A FIELD GUIDE FOR IMPROVING THE CONTEXT OF SCHOOLING

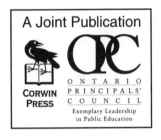

A Joint Publication

CORWIN PRESS

ONTARIO PRINCIPALS' COUNCIL
Exemplary Leadership in Public Education

D1063548

WITHDRAWN

CORWIN PRESS
A SAGE Publications Company
Thousand Oaks, CA 91320

For information:

Corwin Press
A Sage Publications Company
2455 Teller Road
Thousand Oaks, California 91320
www.corwinpress.com

Sage Publications Ltd.
1 Oliver's Yard
55 City Road
London EC1Y 1SP
United Kingdom

Sage Publications India Pvt. Ltd.
B-42, Panchsheel Enclave
Post Box 4109
New Delhi 110 017 India

Printed in the United States of America.

Library of Congress Cataloging-in-Publication Data

Fullan, Michael.
Learning places : a field guide for improving the context
of schooling / Michael Fullan, Clif St. Germain.
p. cm.
"A joint publication with the Ontario Principal's Council."
Includes index.
ISBN 1-4129-4232-2 (cloth : alk. paper)—ISBN 1-4129-4233-0(pbk. : alk. paper)
1. School improvement programs. I. St. Germain, Clif.
II. Ontario Principal's Council. III. Title.
LB2822.8.F848 2006
371.2—dc22

                                                            2006045497

This book is printed on acid-free paper.

06 07 08 09 10 10 9 8 7 6 5 4 3 2 1

Acquisitions Editor:	Robert D. Clouse
Editorial Assistants:	Jingle Vea and Jessica Wochna
Production Editor:	Jenn Reese
Interior Design:	Jennifer Eckstein and Debbi Smith
Typesetters:	Debbi Smith and C&M Digitals (P) Ltd.
Proofreader:	Joyce Li
Indexer:	Karen McKenzie
Cover Designer:	Michael Dubowe
Photos:	Bonita Waesche

CONTENTS

SHAPING SCHOOLWIDE CONTEXTS

SECTION A

IMPROVING CLASSROOM TEACHING

SECTION B

SUSTAINING PASSION AND COMMITMENT

SECTION C

AUTHOR TO READER

Michael Fullan

Thirty–five years ago I wrote my first serious article as a young academic. It was entitled "An overview of the innovative process and the user." At the time, much of the research focused on innovations; I wanted to focus on the people using the innovations. This led to a career-long pursuit of attempting to get at the meaning of educational change. As I worked through the years I realized that we couldn't make progress if we were only interested in individual meaning. The key to large-scale, deeper reform was embedded in the question of how to obtain shared meaning on a wider and wider scale.

As an academic, I spend 80% of my time working with practitioners-teachers, principals, district staff, staff developers, and lately policy makers and politicians. Rather I should say that I work with particular kinds of practitioners—those who want to make a difference not only in their own bailiwicks, but also on the system as a whole.

Increasingly I have been impressed (and frustrated) by the tremendous amount of pent-up passion and pent-up potential that exist in school systems. Many educators want to break out and make a qualitative difference beyond their own classrooms and immediate settings. Some, if they are frustrated for too long in this endeavor, give up and become cynical. Others experience the excitement of making a difference but find that it does not last beyond the tenure of the group with whom they are working. Most, however, no matter what the frustration never give up; they believe intuitively that better things can and should happen—even if they do not know how.

In various partnerships across the world I have been part of helping to create major breakthroughs in individual schools, districts, and in a few cases, entire states. We are getting a taste of what might be possible. It is a tantalizing proposition: literacy and numeracy of students, for example, improve significantly but then level off or plateau; leadership flourishes, especially with leaders helping to develop other leaders but then it wanes when conditions change.

The books I have written capture much of this journey. They describe and extrapolate on the major themes: *The New Meaning of Educational Change*; the *What's Worth Fighting For* trilogy (with Andy Hargreaves); the *Change Forces* trilogy; and what turned out to be a trilogy on leadership: *Leading in a Culture of Change*, *The Moral Imperative of School Leadership*, and *Leadership and Sustainability*. In one of my latest books I team up with Peter Hill and Carmel Crévola to see what it would take to achieve qualitatively greater *Breakthroughs* in education reform (Fullan, Hill, & Crévola, 2006).

Yet, we still have too much pent-up passion and potential. The longer it stays pent-up, the more it dissipates. Passion needs fuel; potential needs to be exercised.

Learning Places is about passion and potential out of the gates. It is about capturing the hearts and minds of all educators. It is a paradox that systems change when people within systems begin to team up and change. People need ideas, tools, opportunities, and other outlets to get started. We believe that the power to change lies closer to ourselves than we realize. It needs to be activated and supported.

I have always teamed up with people who wanted to do more—more than other people thought possible. Along the way I meet some people who are downright irrepressible. I like those who are incorrigibly action-oriented with a reflective twist. This is how I came to join Clif St. Germain. (How could you not work with a guy named "saint," and one whose first name is short one "f" as if it fell over the edge of what the name signifies?)

Clif has done most of the things we recommend in this Field Guide. But he has only done them in a few situations. I, myself, have lately worked with large systems on what I call the "tri-level solution"—what has to happen at the school and community level as one of the trio; the district or regional level as the mid-tri; and the state or policy level as the third level. We have had some success but have not gone deeply enough to reach the hearts and minds of most people at the school and community level.

Learning Places says that with the right ideas and tools all of us can burst outward to change the very contexts within which we work. We can do it; we just need to know how to get started. And the more we learn the how, the more clear and compelling the why becomes.

Learning Places *is, after all, both a point of departure and a destination.*

AUTHOR TO READER

Clif St. Germain

Some people dream of writing the next great novel, others dream of inventing things. Not me. I dream about good schools—happy, bustling, productive schools. I can't think of anything more beautiful. Nor can I remember a time when I wasn't thinking about better ways to unleash the power of passion and commitment I see in the eyes of good teachers. That's why the opportunity to work with Michael Fullan on this Field Guide is, for me, a dream come true. Michael sees deeply into schools. His work is about creating circumstances that enable schools (and school systems) to initiate and sustain their own development.

As I reflect upon my 30 years in schools, especially the 15 years I served as principal of a troubled elementary school, and later a large secondary school, I am reminded of how the circumstances of our daily schedules always seemed to favor a resignation to our present reality. However, in spite of those circumstances, whenever we mustered the courage to set aside our distress (and our dependence on the larger system) and instead made time to talk to each other about improving our teaching, good things happened. By looking deeply at what we were doing, and then taking action on behalf of our students, we found ways to experience the rewards of working with young learners.

In my first appointment as principal, parents wanted the school to be a happy place where children were engaged in relevant learning. This simple mission guided instructional decisions and gave purpose to efforts to improve the school environment. Without going through the usual bureaucratic channels, the faculty threw caution to the winds and painted a rainbow on the front of the school whose stucco walls had not been patched or painted for more than a decade. We became known as the "rainbow school," and the rainbow became the school's emblem, a symbol of our many differences joined together to create something beautiful.

Long before it was popular we recognized the power of professional development. We applied for and were granted special permission to enact an alternative schedule to extend the teaching day four days a week, curtail the teaching day one day a week, and provide time for teachers to refine the daily routines of the school. During this professional development block, teachers discussed student academic profiles, aligned curriculum to standards, shared best-practice teaching strategies and decided upon a future course of action. In sum, we examined every aspect of the school in light of our belief that people learn best in purposeful, validating, and, happy environments. We also discovered that when it comes to learning, the paths to success are as varied as the kids. And even though most of our students were predicted to be low performers, their achievement scores showed otherwise.

Although the circumstances were quite different in my second assignment as principal, similar priorities guided our actions. This large, comprehensive high school, popularized as an academic magnet, was achieving below acceptable standards. Fighting, class cutting, and student surliness were common occurrences.

PURPOSEFULNESS
COLLEGIALITY
PERSISTENCE

Once again, our shared set of priorities and our strong conviction to create the best school possible led to solutions. Parents, teachers, and students agreed that a rigorous academic program in an environment of collegiality was our goal. Therefore, we were guided by three principles: (1) purposefulness, (2) collegiality, and (3) persistence. We later wrote handbooks, course outlines, and standards for excellence in each discipline. We stressed visually pleasing classrooms, honored diversity of thought, and rewarded curiosity, divergent thinking, and questioning. We also instituted schoolwide instructional support programs and created art whenever and wherever we could. We even had the audacity to connect a sound system to the public address system and played symphonic music as students changed classes.

The success of these two schools and the processes we used to reinvent them are now well documented. The elementary school, part of a longitudinal study over the tenure of five principals, was recognized as a model learning community during a presentation at the American Educational Research Association. The high school was named a "National School of Excellence." The contagious momentum we created in both schools was not extraordinary; it is available to all who have the courage to work for it.

PREFACE

"What's all this fuss about a school improvement plan? Let's just complete the forms and get back to teaching our kids."

"We don't have time to rehash what we are doing. Our school is orderly and calm; our classrooms are busy, and students who work hard do well; that's all that really matters."

SOUND FAMILIAR?

This is the conversation of a faculty that has not yet experienced the energizing and empowering effects of a school that is organized to make learning contagious. Faced with the frustrations and challenges of modern schooling, this faculty defends the status quo. Thus, opportunities to positively influence each other and their students go begging.

If you recognize the limitations of this type of thinking or you want to know what you can do to empower yourself and others to create enthusiasm and energy for progress, this book is for you. Not intended as a theoretical review of the literature on school change, *Learning Places* is a field guide, a tool for focusing attention on the kinds of choices that schools must make if they are to create places of learning. As such, *Learning Places* is a book of questions that good schools ask themselves, a book of challenging opportunities for uncovering the best in a school with the intention of making it better, a book designed to advance the progress of any school that has the courage to look deeply at what it does. It is our belief that the intangibles of change that make future development more likely are created in those moments when a school faculty looks deeply at what it does on a daily basis.

Today we know that schools are living entities that grow and develop holistically. We also know that when it comes to teaching young people, little things are often big things. As the current literature on school change confirms, student success is more likely in schools that unify every aspect of the school around supportive, schoolwide practices that emphasize learning. These schoolwide practices are the context of a school. They include everything from the bell schedules to how people treat each other on a daily basis. Contexts are not things we study; they are what we do. They range from daily routines to how schools solve their problems. And they are well within any school's power to change.

Success conforms to the way we pursue it.

Drawing attention to the context of the school, the actual practices through which learning "takes place," helps people uncover new possibilities for improvement. For example, providing student mentors for students who are having difficulty is a recommended contextual element of an effective school program. Having discovered that successful schools offer this type of support to students, a school that does not is faced with a dilemma. It might solve the dilemma by deciding that other programs are more suitable for students or by resolving that study halls would benefit more students; making these choices is a critical component of the improvement process.

We chose the title *Learning Places* because all schools are places. They are concrete and now. Some schools, however, are more than places—they are learning places; they are organized to infuse learning in every nook and cranny of the school. They pay attention to what they do. By grappling with the elements of the school that focus attention on learning, these schools generate the social cohesion that makes future development more likely.

Each chapter in *Learning Places* represents a plan for moving from collective empowerment to action. Chapter 1 establishes the framework of *Learning Places* and the orientation for using the guide as a tool for change. Successive chapters delve into the substance of the journey by helping readers to recognize and shape the important academic, physical, and social contexts of the school (chapters 2, 3, 4, 5); to better incorporate and share mindful classroom practices (chapters 6, 7, 8, 9, 10); and to sustain passion and commitment through professional development (chapters 11, 12).

There are lots to do, so we have a powerful practical message: start with any chapter that you can use to energize your present improvement initiatives and branch out to others as you progress. Don't worry about doing everything at once. Start small, think big. Don't wait for the system to get its act together. Lead by example.

ACKNOWLEDGMENTS

Corwin Press gratefully acknowledges the contributions of the following reviewers:

Nic Cooper
Principal
Saline Middle School
Saline, MI

Tyrone Olverson
Principal
Lincoln Heights Elementary School
Cincinnati, OH

Michelle Gayle
Principal
Griffin Middle School
Tallahassee, FL

Ray Van Dyke
Principal
Kipps Elementary School
Blacksburg, VA

Barry Knight
Principal
Palmetto Middle School
Williamston, SC

Teri White
Principal
Dayton High School
Dayton, NV

Anita M. Micich
Principal
Roosevelt High School
Des Moines, IA

Rosemarie Young
Principal
Watson Lane Elementary School
Louisville, KY

ABOUT THE AUTHORS

Michael Fullan is Professor of Policy Studies at the Ontario Institute of Education, University of Toronto. He is recognized as an international authority on education reform. His ideas for managing change are used in many countries, and his books have been published in several languages. His latest books are *The Moral Imperative of School Leadership, Leadership & Sustainability, Learning Places* (with Clif St. Germain), and *Beyond Turnaround Leadership*. In April 2004, he was appointed Special Adviser on Education to the Premier and Minister of Education in Ontario. He is currently engaged in several systemwide reforms in Ontario, Australia, England, and the United States.

Clif St. Germain has spent three decades helping schools and other organizations design learning environments that maximize individual potential. He received his PhD in Curriculum and Instruction at the University of Texas at Austin, served as principal in two model schools, and now works as an author, lecturer, consultant, and director of The Center for Academic Excellence in Mandeville, Louisiana. Clif also designs learning materials for struggling students and helps school leaders create programs that improve learner performance. He consults with school districts and business leaders across the country to promote learning, leadership, and personal development. His book, *StudyWhiz™*, teaches a learning process that deepens student engagement and organizes information for collaborative thinking and learning.

CHAPTER ONE: BUILDING ON STRENGTHS

ESSENTIAL QUESTION:

What does our current level of organizational competence tell us about promising areas for growth?

BIG IDEA — SUCCESS IS INTENTIONAL.

Nothing in the world can take the place of persistence.

— Calvin Coolidge

This book is about empowering people to constantly reframe the essential elements of their school for the better. It provides two powerful forces for doing this kind of work: one is **conceptual** and the other is **methodological**. In this chapter, we introduce these two forces as essential guides to action, and we use them throughout the book. As you learn to use these forces to create adaptive strategies for coming together in positive ways, you will move closer to creating a place of learning that is self-reliant and sustainable, a place of learning that you helped shape.

MINDSHIFT: *Schoolwide factors shape and condition individual classroom success.*

If we have learned anything from the major school reform initiatives of the last decade it is this: Schools improve from the inside out. What this means is that change efforts must be personalized to fit the context of the individual school if they are to have a chance to take root. Successful schools know this lesson. They come together all the time to identify what's good about the school and celebrate it. As part of this celebration, they make plans to alter those parts of the school that keep them from achieving their goals. Because successful schools are ever vigilant to "look round" and pay attention to what they are really like inside, they are better prepared to improve what they do.

In this Field Guide we invite you to look at your school in new ways. Provided here are templates and strategies that focus attention upon how your school is organized for learning. Used appropriately, these templates and strategies get right to the heart of the change process: deciding and acting together.

A successful school improves because it is always learning. It is a Learning Place. *Learning Places*, because they are full of interesting and challenging opportunities to enrich our understanding of the world, like the world, are also places that are fluid. In *Learning Places* success is, by design, more prevalent than failure. Teachers and students are validated and affirmed every day for the quality of their work and neither are afraid to make mistakes. All people in the school community share in success.

A thousand good intentions are no match for a positive act.

— Allen Wheelis

The problem is that most schools are not the learning places we just described. But they could be! In this Field Guide we will provide the conceptual and practical tools that you need to make your school come alive.

This Field Guide provides tools and activities that lead the reader through several phases of dialogue, self-assessment, collaborative decision making, and experimentation with what matters most in terms of becoming a learning place. In a combination of activities involving inquiry and action, this Field Guide seeks to make this journey both purposeful and professionally gratifying.

Figure 1 displays the conceptual mind-set that will be required. It involves focusing on three themes and their synergistic interrelatedness. Essentially moving to new and better schools involves Shaping Schoolwide Contexts, Radically Improving Classroom Teaching, and Sustaining Passion and Commitment. The 12 chapters indicated in Figure 1 pursue in depth these three crucial components of success.

Figure 1

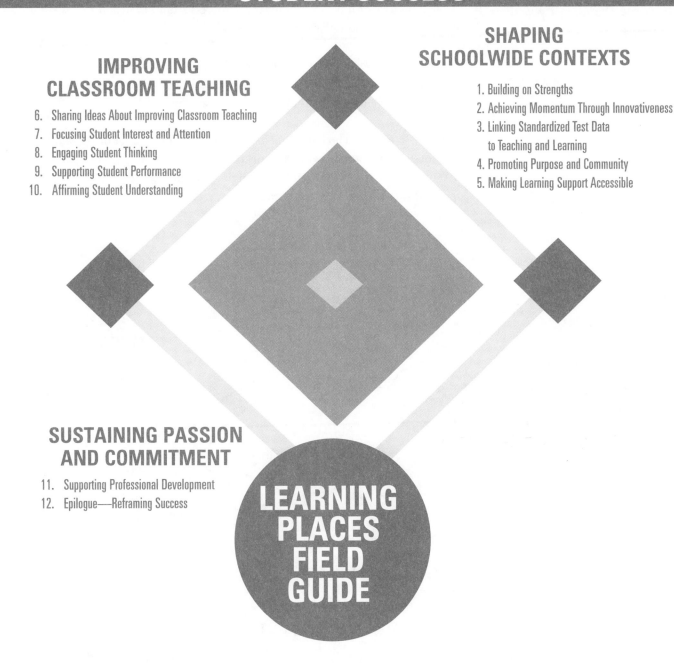

STUDENT SUCCESS

IMPROVING CLASSROOM TEACHING

6. Sharing Ideas About Improving Classroom Teaching
7. Focusing Student Interest and Attention
8. Engaging Student Thinking
9. Supporting Student Performance
10. Affirming Student Understanding

SHAPING SCHOOLWIDE CONTEXTS

1. Building on Strengths
2. Achieving Momentum Through Innovativeness
3. Linking Standardized Test Data to Teaching and Learning
4. Promoting Purpose and Community
5. Making Learning Support Accessible

SUSTAINING PASSION AND COMMITMENT

11. Supporting Professional Development
12. Epilogue—Reframing Success

LEARNING PLACES FIELD GUIDE

Concepts and tools are flip sides of the same Learning Places coin. Concepts without tools are great ideas with no means of getting anywhere. Tools without ideas are mindless. Together they bring out the best in each other. Good tools force greater clarity of thinking; good ideas sharpen the precision of tools, and more than that, they indicate the conditions under which the tool should and should not be used.

TOOLS OF CHANGE

The components of this Field Guide are designed to move the reader through a series of linked activities that progress from discussion to observation, to action planning and beyond.

Concepts, even powerful ones like those in Figure 1, do not develop on their own. For this journey, you will also need critical methods for moving to new destinations. We call these Tools of Change (see Figure 2).

Using these tools, each chapter mediates a specific inquiry about the subtle and not-so-subtle attributes of schools that significantly impact student learning and provide wonderful, challenging, and fulfilling work opportunities for teachers and principals.

Become the lesson you would teach; be what you would have others become.

—Adapted from Gandhi

Figure 2

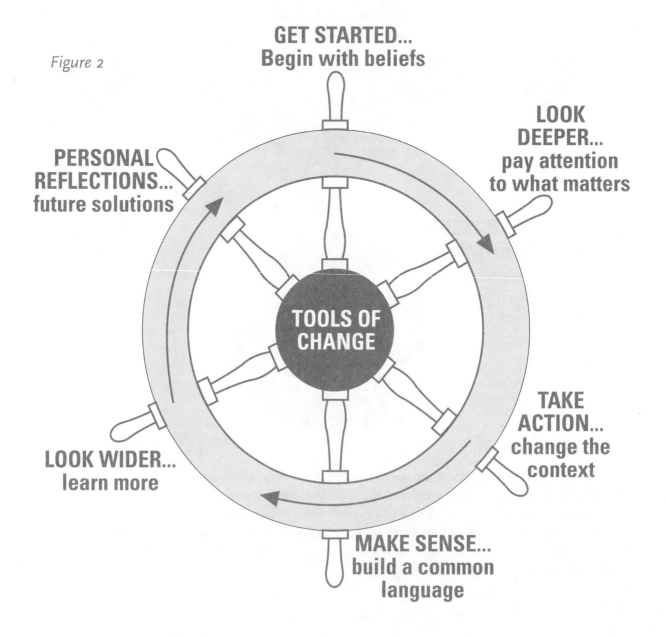

GET STARTED...
Begin with beliefs

LOOK DEEPER...
pay attention to what matters

PERSONAL REFLECTIONS...
future solutions

TOOLS OF CHANGE

TAKE ACTION...
change the context

LOOK WIDER...
learn more

MAKE SENSE...
build a common language

GETTING STARTED is made actionable in this Field Guide using a **READ REACT SHARE** learning strategy. Readers are encouraged to preview the questions, make personal notes, discuss these notes with colleagues, and then form collective judgments that "jump-start" purposeful action. These judgments are the nuts and bolts of shared purpose. This dialogue is intended to "set the stage" for meaningful inquiry, which is the next step in the improvement process.

In schools where the challenges are formidable (and those where they are not), there is a temptation to skip the Getting Started phase of school reform. The familiar "been there; done that" is the killer phrase of choice for opinion leaders who do not understand the importance of constantly shaping the conditions that surround them.

LOOKING DEEPER is a Field Guide activity designed to draw the reader ever closer to specific examples of the school's present state of operation. Looking Deeper connects observations to future action. The Looking Deeper template is usually presented in checklist format for use as an observation tool. Looking Deeper gives more specificity to what is happening or what is not happening in the school. Looking Deeper always generates positive energy because it gives people an opportunity to validate existing accomplishments.

TAKING ACTION is a suggested group activity designed to lead faculty members and interested volunteers to their own informed judgments about an appropriate course of action. Each Taking Action activity will involve some form of job-embedded experimentation coupled with a decision-making process. Taking Action makes public our commitment to change the context of the school for the better.

REVISITING WHAT WE STAND FOR AND QUESTIONING THE FIT BETWEEN WHAT WE BELIEVE AND WHAT WE DO IS FUNDAMENTAL TO ANY IMPROVEMENT PROCESS.

MAKING SENSE is a glossary of ideas and strategies presented in each chapter. It is designed to give further specificity to ideas and options for changing the conditions of learning present in the school. Readers are encouraged to use the Making Sense component of the Field Guide to build a common language for sharing ideas with others in grade-level meetings, study groups, and faculty planning sessions. Ideally, interested faculty members lead discussions about how a particular strategy or idea might further efforts to improve the school.

LOOKING WIDER is an invitation to learn from recently published books and resources that pertain to each chapter's topic. Intended for use in faculty retreats, study groups, and action research projects that take self-study to the next level of complexity, the references listed here contain substantive information for readers wishing to investigate promising research related to each chapter's topic.

PERSONAL REFLECTIONS is a journaling activity that helps the reader formulate insights into what has been learned and how it can be used to foster continued improvements in the future. Each chapter closes with an opportunity for writing. By writing our personal views about each topic, we create an important bridge between knowing and future action. Readers are asked to write their journal notes in the form of personal experience. The template for journal notes will guide this process.

Each of the aforementioned components can be used independently to form a reasoned basis for appropriate action. Each is intended to lead the reader to personal ideas about how the school might be improved. They are also designed to prompt collaborative dialogue, optimism, and creative problem solving. Shared in an honest attempt to find a better way to orchestrate the many interconnected routines and traditions of a school, these components help practitioners direct their attention and guarantee that they are touching all of the bases.

Used as a system of inquiry, with each connected to the other, the tools of change described here place a particular school with its specific differences at the center of inquiry. In a real sense, because time is always problematic when it comes to school reform, a field guide is only as good as its power to focus attention on the most relevant, actionable information.

It is time to establish the new contexts we need. The ideas and practices we suggest are within the grasp of all of us. We don't need to wait for someone else to improve our lot. It won't happen. The paradox of large-scale fundamental change is that it must be created by individuals and small groups who accomplish real change on the ground. It is time then to change the journey. And you, the reader, can use this Field Guide to create your own dynamic Learning Place.

The central theme of this field guide is that schools and school systems develop best when the people in them are willing to question how they embed learning into all aspects of the school's daily routines. By becoming more aware of a school's habitual ways of organizing for learning and questioning if these habits serve their purposes, schools set into motion a cascade of events that build social cohesion and set the stage for future growth and development.

SEVERAL OPTIONS FOR USING THIS FIELD GUIDE TO STRUCTURE AND ENRICH AN INDIVIDUAL SCHOOL'S SELF-STUDY ARE AS FOLLOWS:

OPTION ONE

Use this book as a guide for a schoolwide faculty study project. Interested faculty members can form study groups to (1) survey the contents of the guide, (2) select one of the three major themes of inquiry, (3) work together to complete suggested activities, and (4) share their recommendations for improving specific elements of the school, its contexts, for the better.

OPTION TWO

Designate a team of interested faculty members or administrators to join teams from "sister schools" to meet regularly to share ideas and "field-tested" strategies for improvement. Assign a section of the Field Guide for completion and then have teams meet to share insights and promising options for shaping the context of schooling for the better.

OPTION THREE

Assign a departmental chairperson in secondary schools and a grade-level chairperson in elementary schools to meet regularly with members of the department using the Field Guide activities to generate dialogue and suggested improvements for their department or grade-level group.

OPTION FOUR

Be creative and design your own "best use" for the Field Guide.

Any place that anyone can learn something useful from someone with experience is an educational institution.

—Al Capp

GETTING STARTED

The following **read-react-share activity** is designed to generate a "fast facts" profile of your school's existing level of operational competence.

It highlights faculty perceptions of the school's strengths and shortcomings.

Directions:
1. *Convene a study group or committee interested in using the Field Guide to generate new ways of seeing, talking about, and solving your school's problems.*
2. *Begin the process by completing the survey charts on the following pages.*
3. *Discuss and summarize committee responses.*
4. *Use these responses to select specific chapters in the Field Guide that are particularly relevant to your school's needs. (See Essential Questions for further clarification.)*
5. *Have fun improving your school and learning together.*

Each chapter of the Field Guide will lead the reader through several phases of inquiry and decision making as follows:

- Reflecting upon and shaping beliefs about the existing conditions of the school program (Getting Started)

- Verifying beliefs in action using observation data (Looking Deeper)

- Selecting promising options and involving other faculty members in implementation projects (Taking Action)

- Further clarifying issues (Making Sense)

- Expanding inquiry to the literature (Looking Wider)

- Capturing reflections and representing outcomes (Personal Reflections)

NOTE WELL:

Before getting started, let us highlight one crucial fact. *Learning Places* is about "learning in context." It is about job-embedded learning where workshops, courses, and policies are only external inputs. Such inputs do not matter unless they are coupled with day-to-day learning in school and district cultures. Judith Little put it best in her early studies of collegiality: imagine that you would become a better teacher, just by virtue of the fact that you were on the staff of a particular school (or imagine the opposite).

List everything you would tell a prospective parent or student about your school's unique features: its programs, learning-centered routines, achievements, and campus.

What would you say to a colleague about aspects of the school that would warrant attention?

STRENGTHS	CONCERNS
UNIQUE PROGRAMS:	
LEARNING-CENTERED ROUTINES:	
ACHIEVEMENTS:	
CAMPUS FEATURES:	

SECTION A
SHAPING SCHOOLWIDE CONTEXTS: CHAPTERS 2, 3, 4, 5

List everything you would say to a visiting teacher about effective teaching practices they might observe in classrooms.

What would you say to a colleague about your concerns about the quality of teaching innovations in your school?

STRENGTHS	CONCERNS
Effective Teaching Practices:	

SECTION B
MINDFUL TEACHING: CHAPTERS 6, 7, 8, 9, 10

List everything you would say to a business partner or distant administrator about projects and faculty development initiatives that have had positive effects upon student learning.

What would you tell a colleague about recent Professional Development initiatives aimed at improving teaching capacity and innovativeness among faculty members?

PROMISING STRATEGIES	CONCERNS
Professional Development Initiatives:	Sustaining Passion and Commitment:

BASED UPON THIS INFORMAL SURVEY DATA, LIST SEVERAL STRATEGIC PRIORITIES THAT MERIT CONSIDERATION:

-
-
-
-

SECTION C
SUSTAINING PASSION AND COMMITMENT: CHAPTERS 11, 12

CREATING A LEARNING PLACE

PERSONAL REFLECTIONS:

Jot down your main learnings from Chapter 1

CHAPTER TWO: ACHIEVING MOMENTUM THROUGH INNOVATIVENESS

ESSENTIAL QUESTION:

How can we use change knowledge to cultivate and model innovativeness—the capacity to develop leadership behaviors in others?

BIG IDEA — THE PROCESS OF ACQUIRING NEW KNOWLEDGE AND CAPACITY IS EMBEDDED MORE IN THE ACTUAL DOING OF THE TASK AND LESS IN FORMAL TRAINING. (Pfeffer & Sutton, 2002)

Like all chapters in this Field Guide, this one can be used as a stand-alone exercise to deepen your knowledge about change or it can be used in connection with other chapters. Change, of course, permeates all aspects of Learning Places whether we are Changing Schoolwide Contexts or Improving Classroom Teaching, or Sustaining Passion and Commitment.

The voyage of the best ship is a zigzag line of a hundred tracks.

—— Ralph Waldo Emerson

Nonetheless it is important to think about change in its own right. Many a great idea has been shattered against the walls of change barriers. Change knowledge concerns a proven body of ideas and actions that are known to help or hinder the likelihood of making progress. The first and overriding thing to know is that change knowledge is not about particular innovations—being an expert in literacy for example. Rather it is about innovativeness—how to achieve movement or continuous improvement.

Let's try a teaser first. Everyone knows that ownership or shared vision is crucial to success. But did you know that shared vision is more a *product* of a quality process than it is a precondition of moving forward? Our change knowledge tool kit contains six big ideas. As usual, we present them first as concepts so that the reader can grasp them cognitively and then we use the action change tools to go deeper into your Learning Place.

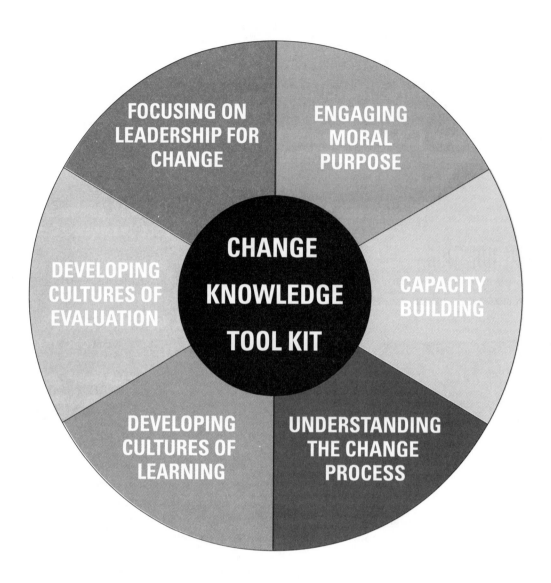

SIX BIG IDEAS ABOUT CHANGE

ENGAGING MORAL PURPOSE

The first overriding principle concerns knowledge about the why of change, namely, moral purpose. At a fundamental level, moral purpose in educational change is about improving society through improving educational systems and thus the learning of all citizens.

In education, moral purpose involves a commitment to raising the bar and closing the gap in student achievement, for example, increasing literacy for all with special attention to those most disadvantaged. There is a wide gap, particularly in some countries between groups at the bottom and those at the top. Thus, schools need to "raise the floor" by figuring out how to speed up the learning of those who are at the bottom for whom the school system has been less effective.

Improving overall literacy achievement is directly associated with economic productivity in a country. In countries where the gap between high and low performance of students is reduced, the economic health and well-being of citizens is measurably better. Moral purpose, then, is about student learning at levels not before achieved. It is also about how people treat each other—caring, but also demanding expectations to do better. And it is about whether we contribute to the amelioration of the social environment. Learning Places are not just for us but also for schools around us. We all have responsibility for contributing to and learning from other schools, not just for focusing narrowly on our own situation.

In change knowledge, moral purpose is not just a goal, but more important, is a process of engaging educators, community leaders, and society as a whole in the moral purpose of reform. If moral purpose is front and center, the remaining five drivers become additional forces for enacting moral purpose.

What is worth fighting for is not to allow our schools to be negative by default, but to make them positive by design.

2 CAPACITY BUILDING

The second driver is capacity building, which involves policies, strategies, resources, and other actions designed to increase the collective power of people to move the system forward (schools, districts, state levels). This will involve the development (collective development) of new "knowledge, skills, and competencies," new resources (time, ideas, materials), and new 'shared identity and motivation' to work together for greater change. At the school level, then, new competencies, enhanced resources, and great collective motivation need to be mobilized.

Capacity is crucial because it is often the missing element even when people are in agreement about the need for change. For example, teachers and principals must develop new skills and increased commitment in the face of inevitable obstacles (see the third driver) to improve literacy. Similarly, in the case of new technologies not only must educators acquire new skills and understandings, they must integrate technology into curriculum, teaching and learning, and the assessment of learning.

Capacity building, we should stress, is a "collective" phenomenon. Whole schools must increase their capacity as groups. This is difficult because it involves working together in new ways.

"There can be no improvement in schools without good teachers."

The ideas in this Field Guide provide the resources for developing new ways to work collectively.

In addition to individual and collective capacity as defined by increased knowledge, resources, and motivation, organizational capacity involves improvements in the infrastructure. The infrastructure consists of agencies at the local, regional, and state levels that can deliver new capacity in the system such as training, consultancy, and other support.

3 UNDERSTANDING THE CHANGE PROCESS

Understanding the change process is a big driver because it cuts across all elements. It is also difficult and frustrating to grasp because it requires leaders to take into account factors that they would rather not have to stop and deal with. They would rather lay out the purpose and plan and get on with it. Change doesn't work that way.

For change to work you need the energy, ideas, commitment, and "ownership" of all those implicated in implementing improvements. This is perplexing because the urgency of problems does not allow for long-term "ownership development" (in fact, more leisurely strategies do not produce greater ownership anyway).

Here are five things you should know about the process of change—they all underscore the point that change is a process, not an event.

> i. Strategizing vs. strategy
>
> ii. Pressure and support
>
> iii. Know about the implementation dip
>
> iv. Understand the fear of change
>
> v. Be persistent and resilient

STRATEGIZING:

There is a great temptation to develop the complete strategic plan and then allocate mechanisms of accountability and support in order to implement it. This leads to the first lesson in the change process: The strategic plan is an innovation; it is not innovativeness.

We need strategy and strategic ideas, but above all, we need to think of the evolution of change plans as a process of shaping and reshaping ideas and actions. Henry Mintzberg, in his 2004 critique of existing MBA programs (*Managers not MBAs*), captures this idea precisely:

> *Strategy is an interactive process, not a two-step sequence; it requires continual feedback between thought and action.... Strategists have to be in touch; they have to know what they are strategizing about; they have to respond and react and adjust, often allowing strategies to emerge, step-by-step. In a word, they have to* learn. (p. 55)

Effective change is more about strategizing than strategy; it is a process. The more leaders practice strategizing, the more they hone their scientific and intuitive knowledge of the change process.

 PRESSURE AND SUPPORT:

The second element of understanding change dynamics concerns the realization that all deep change requires the combination and integration of "pressure and support."

There is a great deal of inertia in social systems, which means that new forces are required to change direction. These new forces involve the judicious use of pressure and support.

Pressure means ambitious targets, transparent evaluation and monitoring, calling upon moral purpose, and the like. Support involves developing new competencies, access to new ideas, and more time for learning and collaboration.

The more that pressure and support become seamless, the more effective the change process at getting things to happen. As the six drivers of change begin to operate in concert, pressure and support, in effect, get built into the ongoing culture of interaction. Because pressure and support in balance are nonnegotiable components of Learning Places, we subscribe to ensuring that both get "owned" by the group. This develops the most powerful accountability there is: internal accountability.

 THE IMPLEMENTATION DIP:

The third aspect of understanding the change process is to know that all eventual successful change proceeds through an "implementation dip."

Since change involves grappling with new beliefs and understandings, and new skills, competences, and behaviors, it is inevitable that it will not go smoothly in the early stages of implementation (even if there has been pre-implementation preparation). This applies to any individual, but is much more complex when (as is always the case) many people are involved simultaneously.

Knowledge of the implementation dip has helped in two important ways in our work with change initiatives. First, it has brought out into the open and given people a label for what are normal, common experiences, namely, that all changes worth their salt involve a somewhat awkward learning period.

The tendency to anticipate trouble from the system is one of the most frequent and major obstacles to trying new ideas.

Second, it has resulted in our being able to reduce the period of awkwardness. By being aware of the problem, we are able to use strategies (support, training, etc.) that reduce the implementation dip from (in the case of school change) three years to half that time. This obviously depends on the starting conditions and complexity of the change, but the point is that without knowledge of the implementation dip, problems persist and people give up without giving the idea a chance.

Shorter implementation dips are more tolerable and once gains start to be made earlier, motivation increases. Note that motivation is increasing (or not) during the implementation process. This is a sign of a quality (or poor) change process.

 THE FEAR OF CHANGE:

The fear of change is classical change knowledge. What people need to know from inception is that at the beginning of the change process the losses are specific and tangible (it is clear what is being left behind), but the gains are theoretical and distant. This is so by definition. You cannot realize the gains until you master implementation, and this takes time. More than this, you don't necessarily have confidence that the gains will be attained. It is a theoretical proposition.

Black and Gregersen (2002) talk about "brain barriers" such as the failure to move in new directions even when the direction is clear. The clearer the new vision, the more immobilized people become! Why?

Their answer:

> **The clearer the new vision, the easier it is for people to see all the specific ways in which they will be incompetent and look stupid. Many prefer to be competent at the [old] wrong thing than incompetent at the [new] right thing. (p. 70)**

In other words, an additional element of change process knowledge involves realizing that clear, even inspiring, visions are not sufficient. People need new experiences and reflective learning to become adept and comfortable with "the new right way."

 PERSISTENCE AND RESILIENCE:

Engaging others in the process of change requires not only persistence in order to overcome the inevitable challenges—to keep on going despite setbacks—but it also involves adaptation and problem solving through being flexible enough to incorporate new ideas into strategizing.

Both focus and flexibility are needed.

The concept that captures persistence and flexibility is "resilience." Because change processes are complex, difficult, and frustrating, it requires pushing ahead without being rigid, regrouping despite setbacks, and not being discouraged when progress is slow.

The reason we emphasize persistence and resilience is that people often start with grand intentions and aspirations, but gradually lower them over time in the face of obstacles and in the end achieve precious little.

Thus, armed with change knowledge, people need to approach the change process with a commitment to maintain, even increase, high standards and aspirations. Obstacles should be seen as problems and barriers to be resolved in order to achieve high targets rather than as reasons for consciously not lowering aspirations.

4 DEVELOPING CULTURES OF LEARNING

The fourth driver, cultures of learning, is what our whole Field Guide is about, but we would like to describe it explicitly here. Cultures of learning involve a whole set of strategies designed so that people can learn from each other (the knowledge dimension) and become collectively committed to improvement (the affective dimension). Strategies for learning from each other involve:

- *Developing learning communities at the local, school, and community levels*
- *Learning from other schools, regional and otherwise (lateral capacity building)*

Successful change involves learning during implementation. One of the most powerful drivers of change involves learning from peers, especially those who are further along in implementing new ideas. We can think of such learning inside the school and local community, and across schools or jurisdictions. There is a great deal of practical research within the school that demonstrates the necessity and power of "Professional Learning Communities."

Newmann and his colleagues (2000) identified five components of change capacity within the school that include the development of new knowledge and skills, establishing professional learning communities, program coherence, access to new resources, and principal/school leadership. Schools and their local villages and communities must develop new cultures of learning how to improve.

When school systems establish cultures of learning, they constantly seek and develop teachers' knowledge and skills required to create effective new learning experiences for students. In addition to school and community building, a powerful new strategy is called "lateral capacity building." This strategy involves schools and communities learning from each other within a given district or region and beyond. This widens the pool of ideas and also enhances a greater "we-we" identity beyond one school (Fullan, 2005).

Knowledge sharing and collective identity are powerful forces for positive change, and they form a core component of our change knowledge (i.e., we need to value these aspects and know how to put them into action). Pfeffer and Sutton (2000) reinforce this conclusion in their analysis of the Knowing-Doing Gap. They claim that we should "embed" more of the process of acquiring new knowledge in the actual doing of the task and less in formal training programs that are frequently ineffective (p. 27). Change knowledge has a bias for action. Developing a climate where people learn from each other within and across units, and being preoccupied with turning good knowledge into action is essential. Turning information into actionable knowledge is a social process. Thus, developing learning cultures is crucial. Good policies and ideas take off in learning cultures, and go nowhere in cultures of isolation.

 ## DEVELOPING CULTURES OF EVALUATION

Cultures of evaluation must be coupled with cultures of learning in order to sort out promising from not-so-promising ideas and especially to deepen the meaning of what is learned. As we will see in Chapter 3, one of the highest yield strategies for educational change recently developed is "Assessment for Learning" (not just assessment of learning).

Assessment for learning incorporates:

Accessing/gathering data on student learning

Disaggregating data for more detailed understanding

Developing action plans based on the previous two points in order to make improvements

Articulating and discussing performance with parents, external groups

When schools and school systems increase their collective capacity to engage in ongoing assessment for learning, major improvements are achieved. Several other aspects of evaluation cultures are important including: school-based self-appraisal, meaningful use of external accountability data, and what Jim Collins (2002) found in "great" organizations, namely, a commitment to "confronting the brutal facts," and establishing a culture of disciplined inquiry.

Cultures of evaluation serve external accountability as well as internal data processing purposes. They produce data on an ongoing basis that enables groups to use information for action planning as well as for external accounting (see Black et al., 2003, and Stiggins, 2001).

One other matter, technology has become an enormously necessary and powerful tool in our work on assessment as it makes it possible to access and analyze student achievement data on an ongoing basis, take corrective action, and share best solutions. Developing cultures of evaluation and capacity to use technology for improvement must go hand in hand; both are seriously underdeveloped in most systems we know.

School leadership is all about fostering success in others.

 ## FOCUSING ON LEADERSHIP FOR CHANGE

As might be expected, one of the most powerful lessons for change involves leadership. Here change knowledge consists of knowing what kind of leadership is best for leading productive change. It turns out that high-flying, charismatic leaders look like powerful change agents, but are actually bad for business because too much revolves around themselves.

Leadership, to be effective, must spread throughout the organization. Collins (2002) found that charismatic leaders were negatively associated with sustainability. Leaders of the so-called "great" organizations were characterized by "deep personal humility" and "intense professional will." Collins talks about the importance of leadership that "builds enduring greatness" in the organization, rather than just focusing on short-term results.

To provide a specific illustration, the main mark of school principals at the end of their tenure is not just their impact on the bottom line of student achievement, but rather how many leaders they leave behind who can go even farther. Mintzberg (2004) makes the same point:

> Successful managing is not about one's own success but about fostering success in others. (p. 16)

> While managers have to make decisions, far more important, especially in large networked organizations of knowledge works, is what they do to enhance decision-making capabilities of others. (p. 38)

Change knowledge, then, means avoiding leaders who represent only innovation, and seeking those who represent innovativeness—the capacity to develop leadership in others on an ongoing basis. We need to produce a critical mass of leaders who have change knowledge. Such leaders produce and feed on other leadership through the system. There is no other driver as essential for enduring Learning Places as leadership.

All in all, forcibly put, you cannot create Learning Places without constantly acquiring and honing your repertoire of change knowledge. We have laid out six main drivers of this knowledge base. The reader can attempt cognitively to understand these forces for change, and we highly recommend that people do this directly. But to really deepen one's grasp of the core ideas, one needs to put them into practice and learn by reflective doing. The tools for change in this chapter help do just that.

GETTING STARTED

GETTING STARTED

How has our faculty increased its capacity to develop leadership behaviors in others?

GETTING STARTED

Have teachers experienced the implementation dip? How so?

GETTING STARTED

What makes our school a culture of learning?

LOOKING DEEPER

Directions: Observe your school in action and write descriptions of the six change drivers. Use real, observable examples.

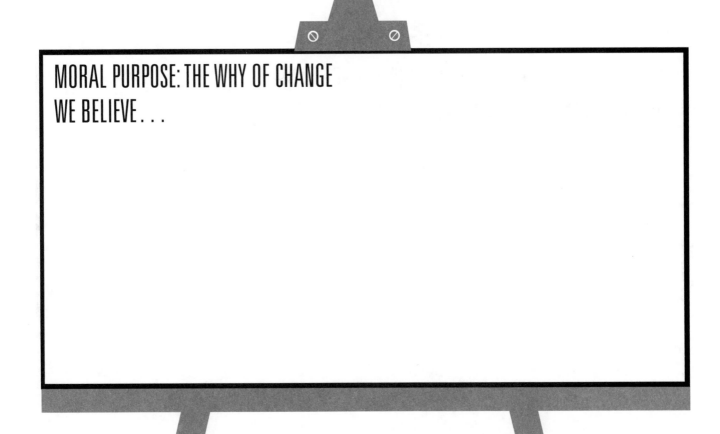

MORAL PURPOSE: THE WHY OF CHANGE
WE BELIEVE...

CAPACITY BUILDING: COLLECTIVE DEVELOPMENT
WE STRIVE TO HELP EACH OTHER BY...

UNDERSTANDING THE CHANGE PROCESS: CHANGE WISDOMS
WE BUILD OWNERSHIP COMMITMENT AND ENERGY BY...

DEVELOPING A CULTURE OF LEARNING: LEARNING FROM EACH OTHER
WE HAVE RECENTLY LEARNED HOW TO . . .

DEVELOPING A CULTURE OF EVALUATION: DATA-DRIVEN ADVOCACY
OUR ACADEMIC PERFORMANCE RESULTS INDICATE THAT . . .

FOCUSING LEADERSHIP FOR CHANGE: FOSTERING SUCCESS IN OTHERS
WE BUILD WIDER CIRCLES OF LEADERSHIP BY . . .

MAKING SENSE

THE VOCABULARY OF ACHIEVING MOMENTUM THROUGH INNOVATIVENESS

CAPACITY BUILDING

involves any action or strategy that increases the collective efficacy of a group to improve student learning for all. It consists of three things being synergized: new knowledge and competencies, enhanced resources, and greater motivation and commitment to make improvements.

COLLECTIVE IDENTITY

is a group of self-image shaped by, but in turn shaping the consciousness of, individual participants. It is best observed in rituals and varied forms of organizational affiliation.

CULTURE OF LEARNING

is a set of beliefs, behaviors, and expectations that collectively affirm that people learn best in a context of challenge and validation, a context that draws people together in purposeful ways.

IMPLEMENTATION DIP

is the early phase of an innovation in which progress is stalled while people grapple with the new knowledge, skills, and understandings required for new breakthroughs.

INNOVATIVENESS

is a contagious state of exploration that creates momentum for program and organizational improvement. Innovativeness involves how to bring about continuous improvement.

KNOWLEDGE SHARING

is an open exchange of information that takes place between people who have a common aim and can work together effectively.

LATERAL CAPACITY BUILDING

is capacity building across different levels of an organization. It can occur within a school, across schools in a district, or even across school districts in a state or county. The evidence suggests that lateral capacity building works best when it has a clear purpose, a means of measuring whether progress is being made in achieving the purpose, a clear evidence-based definition of best practice to inform action, and in all these respects has purposeful leadership.

LEARNING IN CONTEXT

You can't mandate what matters.

Learning in workshops or in courses is learning out of context. It is necessary and helpful, but only to a point. Learning on the job, in the setting in which you work, is where the payoff occurs—because the learning, by definition, is specific to your context. And because it is in context it is *shared* learning making it all the more powerful. Cultures of learning embed learning in context.

MORAL PURPOSE

is a commitment to improve the impact of schooling by making support for learning and challenging content accessible to all students. It also involves being aware of how you treat others (caring plus demanding expectations), and how you treat the social environment by contributing to the growth of other schools.

OWNERSHIP DEVELOPMENT

is a concept that describes a collectively owned and embraced process for improving and sustaining change initiatives. It is more an outcome of a quality process of working together than it is a precondition.

RESILIENCE

is the human capacity (and ability) to face, overcome, become strengthened by, and even be transformed by experiences of difficulty. Resilience is persistence plus flexibility.

STRATEGIZING

is the practice of making sense of the big picture prior to developing a plan to shape and reshape ideas and actions. Strategizing is not a two-step process of developing a strategy and then implementing it, but rather is developing a plan that is then refined by interacting with the situation. Strategizing is dynamic and is shaped and reshaped by attempting to solve problems in order to get greater improvements.

TAKING ACTION

Directions: Create six large posters, one for each of the six change forces discussed in this chapter. Post one poster per month in the faculty lounge and encourage teachers to make comments on it, highlighting specific examples of this change force in action and offering suggestions that can help others take a leadership role in using each change driver to move the school forward.

Rotate posters each month, and after six months summarize the comments for use in a faculty discussion about achieving momentum for change through innovativeness.

MORAL PURPOSE	
Examples	*Suggestions for developing wider circles of leadership*

CAPACITY BUILDING	
Examples	*Suggestions for developing wider circles of leadership*

UNDERSTANDING CHANGE PROCESS

Examples	Suggestions for developing wider circles of leadership

CREATING A CULTURE OF LEARNING

Examples	Suggestions for developing wider circles of leadership

CREATING A CULTURE OF EVALUATION

Examples	Suggestions for developing wider circles of leadership

FOCUSING LEADERSHIP FOR CHANGE

Examples	Suggestions for developing wider circles of leadership

LOOKING WIDER

SUGGESTED READINGS

Abrahamson, Eric, "Change Without Pain," Harvard Business School Press, 2003

Black, J. Stewart, and Gergersen, Hal B., "Leading Strategic Change," Prentice Hall, 2002

Black, P., Harrison, C., Lee, C., Marshall, B., & William, D., "Assessment for Learning in the Classroom," Open University Press, 2004

Block, Peter, "The Answer to How Is Yes," Berrett-Koehler Publishers, 2002

Collins, Jim, "Good to Great," HarperCollins, 2001

Fullan, Michael, "Change Forces With a Vengeance," RoutledgeFarmer, 2003

Fullan, Michael, "The Moral Imperative of School Leadership," Ontario Principals' Council and Corwin Press – A Joint Publication, 2003

Fullan, Michael, "The New Meaning of Educational Change," Teachers College Press, 3rd Edition, 2001

Fullan, Michael and Hargreaves, Andy, "What's Worth Fighting for in Your School," Teachers College Press, 1996

Maxwell, John C., "Developing the Leaders Around You," Thomas Nelson Publishers, 1995

Mintzberg, Henry, "Managers Not MBAs: A Hard Look at the Soft Practice of Managing and Management Development," Berrett-Koehlers Publishers, Inc., 2004

Newmann, F., King, B., and Youngs, P., "Professional Development That Addresses School Capacity," paper presented at the annual meeting of the American Education Research Association

Pfeffer, Jeffrey, and Sutton, Robert I., "The Knowing Doing Gap," Harvard Business School Publishing, 2000

Stiggins, Rick, "New Assessment Beliefs for a New School Mission," in Phi Delta Kappan, September 2004

Vaill, Peter B., "Learning as a Way of Being," Jossey-Bass Publishers, 1996

In the end, an organization is nothing more than the collective capacity of its people to create value.

CREATING A LEARNING PLACE

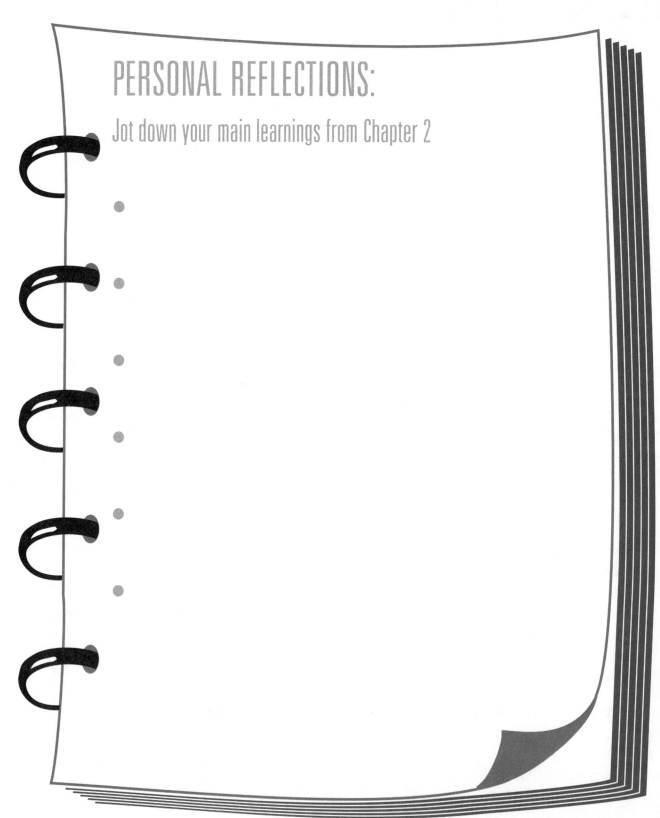

PERSONAL REFLECTIONS:

Jot down your main learnings from Chapter 2

CHAPTER THREE: LINKING STANDARDIZED TEST DATA TO TEACHING AND LEARNING

ESSENTIAL QUESTION:

How can teachers use standardized test data to (1) provide students with relevant academic support, (2) monitor student progress, and (3) determine the extent to which students have the knowledge and skills expected of their age group?

BIG IDEA — INDIVIDUAL STUDENT GROWTH IS THE MEASURE OF CHOICE WHEN ASSESSING LEARNER PERFORMANCE.

A child we know entered kindergarten excited about learning. Like many of her classmates she came to kindergarten after two years of preschool and years of informal teaching by her two educated parents. At the end of the school year all of the children in her class were given a battery of standardized tests to determine their level of academic performance. And to no one's surprise the results indicated that most of the students in this class scored in the highest performance category.

Across town another group of kindergarten children in this school district took the same battery of tests. These children, however, came to school with little preparation for such tests. Their scores after a full year of school were generally in the below-average performance range.

MINDSHIFT: *Understanding the benefits of standardized testing as a tool for improving teaching and learning is a core competency of modern education.*

WHICH CLASS HAD MORE PROGRESS? THE ANSWER: WE DON'T KNOW.

Since 1920 teachers have depended upon standardized tests to determine the extent to which students are prepared to deal with the rigors of specific academic programs. But today the "stakes" are higher. Standardized tests have been drafted into the accountability movement and made public as expected outcomes of schooling.

Although these high-stakes standardized tests dominate accepted accountability practices, because they are commonly reported as aggregate end-state summaries of student achievement, without considerable translation, they do not provide specific guidance as to appropriate conditions for improving individual student performance. The challenge at the school and classroom level is to link standardized test data to promising programs, resources, and teacher behaviors that influence individual student performance for the better. This means using test data to engage students in a dialogue about their present level of performance and searching for ways to improve that performance. It means creating classrooms and schools that are responsive to individual learners. It means integrating standardized test data with teacher-generated assessment indicators such as progress reports, grades, student self-assessments, and classroom performances to create profiles of continuous improvement. And finally, it means placing less emphasis on end-state statistics of performance and more on "in progress" formative indicators of individual student growth and development.

What follows in this chapter are ideas and suggestions for using standardized test data to frame a dialogue between teachers, students, and parents that links effort with learning and success. By incorporating desirable schoolwide conditions and classroom strategies that are promising antecedents to standardized achievement gains, schools guarantee continuous improvement.

Assessment for learning is to assessment of learning what regular physical examinations are to autopsies.

—Doug Reeves

LEARNING-LINKED DATA

Several of the popular standardized tests contain valuable scales teachers can use to provide students and parents with information that can be used to indicate progress toward specific academic goals. These scales provide a treasure trove of data for determining the year-to-year growth of individual students. Standard Scores, for example, are benchmarks for typical performance in each grade. Using Standard Scores, teachers can establish reasonable growth targets for learners that can be (1) linked to specific skills, (2) assessed periodically throughout the school year, and (3) used to determine schoolwide instructional support.

Using Standard Score comparisons, teachers can draw attention to what students have accomplished rather than to what they have not. By charting expected growth for every student and affirming students who meet or exceed personal growth targets, teachers individualize testing success. By taking into account a student's entry level of performance as a basis for comparison, schools also document how much or how little their students are learning. The advocacy role of teaching now involves helping students make sense of these scores in ways that support their continued development.

INDIVIDUAL ACADEMIC PROFILES

Individualized academic profiles help teachers demystify test data and provide students with specific information about their present level of performance. What follows is a step-by-step procedure for using norm-referenced standardized test data to generate academic profiles.

1. *Determine the Developmental Standard Score for the core total or a basic battery subtest as reported on norm-referenced student profiles. The core total (basic battery subtest) is a composite of reading, language, and math performance and therefore reasonably represents overall literacy.*

2. *Establish for each student an entry level of performance and use this score to determine expected levels of growth for one school year. For scores near the median, expected growth will be one year of growth. For below average scores, the expected growth will be 60% of or slightly below average growth. For above-average performance, expected growth will be above average or approximately 40% above-average growth.*

3. *Explain the expected growth for core total to each student and highlight the relationship between reading, language, and math subtests and the core total. Note: Subtest scores that are below the core total scores should be linked to specific skills areas and assessed using alternate assessments throughout the school year. Subtest scores in reading, language, and math should also be used to enroll students in schoolwide instructional support programs such as tutorial programs, mathematics help sessions, or mentor programs.*

4. *When test scores are reported at the end of the year, compute student growth using core total comparisons, validate success, and/or recommend learning support as needed.*

5. *Begin the next school year with a parent information night and share scores and their interpretations.*

NORM-REFERENCED PROFILES

Using the Developmental Standard Score as an index of growth, the average student is predicted to grow 10 months in a given school year, regardless of grade level. Reported as a median score (Md), that point in the distribution where half of the scores are above and half below, a developmental score progression representing typical or average growth over the years of schooling reads as follows:

Kindergarten	130	6th	grade	228
1st grade	150	7th	grade	240
2nd grade	169	8th	grade	250
3rd grade	186	9th	grade	260
4th grade	202	10th	grade	268
5th grade	216	11th	grade	274

The chart above shows the median annual growth for the Core Total subtest of the recently normed Iowa Test of Basic Skills (K–8) and the Iowa Test of Educational Development (9–11). For this subtest, average students, regardless of grade level, are expected to grow the equivalent of one year of schooling in a given school year.

Students whose previous achievement levels are below average would be predicted by the test developers to show less than one year's growth, or an increased growth that is at least 60% of annual growth. Students whose previous achievement levels are above average might be expected to grow up to 40% in excess of one year's growth for each year of schooling. Using this scale, teachers can take advantage of projected growth statistics to compute reasonable goals for improvement for all students.

Teachers are encouraged to begin with a student's previous performance on an overall indicator of growth like the Core Battery Score. The Core Battery is a composite of reading, language, and math subtests. Then compare performance over two or three years to guarantee that every student has a worthwhile, attainable goal for academic growth. Finally, emphasize that by using these comparisons all effortful students can experience the personal satisfaction that accompanies the attainment of a meaningful goal.

For example, if Harold Jackson is an average seventh-grade student who completed sixth grade with a developmental standard score of 228 for this subtest, he would be expected to achieve a score of at least 240 in seventh grade, indicating 12 points of growth. However, if Harold is a below-average student entering seventh grade with a previous score of 210, a more accurate growth target would be between 8 and 12 points or at least 60% of the 12 point expected growth of the average student. Similarly, if Harold is an above-average student, he might be expected to grow approximately 17 points or an additional 5 points beyond the average expected growth.

Charting and interpreting yearly academic growth using the Developmental Standard score provides a context for teachers to reframe success on high-stakes tests by clearly defining the allocation of effort necessary for achieving it.

For schools using Plan and ACT standardized tests as summative measures of student performance, 10th-grade Plan data can also be used to help students identify areas of strength and set reasonable goals for performance on the ACT.

How does our school interpret test data for students and parents?

How does our school use standardized achievement data to encourage individual students to become more effortful learners?

What is our school's response to students who fail to demonstrate appropriate growth and/or mastery on standardized measures of achievement?

LOOKING DEEPER

USING STANINE DATA TO TARGET SCHOOLWIDE INSTRUCTIONAL SUPPORT

Stanine scores indicate a student's relative standing within a group of students in the same grade who were tested at the same time of year. Stanine scores range from a low of 1 to a high of 9, with 1, 2, 3 considered below average; 4, 5, 6 average; and 7, 8, 9 above average.

Stanines used appropriately are yet another learner-friendly statistic. Stanines give teachers immediate cues about the general characteristics and needs of individual learners in each category. These scores are particularly useful for grouping students for instruction and matching students to appropriate schoolwide learning assistance programs. Using stanine comparisons teachers can devise and evaluate schoolwide instructional support programs for every student performance level in the school.

Another strategy for linking test data to teaching and learning is to use stanine data to identify students for schoolwide instructional support programs. Review the following descriptions and suggested interventions for each of the nine stanine classifications. In the space provided, note your school's present instructional support programs for each. (See Making Sense segment at end of this chapter for definitions of unfamiliar terms.)

That evil is half-cured whose cause we know.

—Charles Churchill

VERY LOW PERFORMANCE
STANINES 1 & 2

Students in stanines 1 & 2 most often also score in the lowest range of performance on criterion measures. Stanine 1 performance is equivalent to percentiles 1st–3rd, and stanine 2 is equivalent to percentiles 4th–10th.

Students scoring in the bottom two stanines share similar characteristics and needs as follows:
- Test performance is extremely low.
- Need the most elemental of help: reading support
- Need much more time with a certified teacher in reading instruction
- Need to be encouraged to read for pleasure
- Should be reviewed for special services
- If their scores are supported by other measures and their performance in school is questionable, expecting these students to reach the average range of performance in one year of schooling is not supportable.
- Their success is best measured by the acquisition of basic literacy skills and year-to-year incremental gains in academic performance.

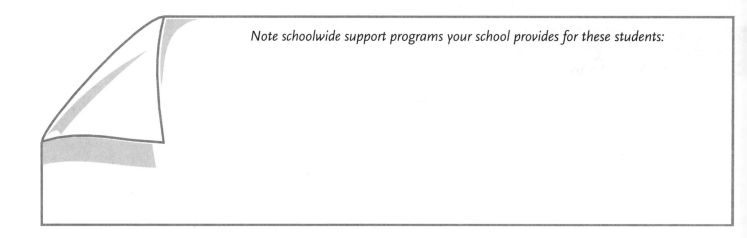

Note schoolwide support programs your school provides for these students:

WELL BELOW-AVERAGE PERFORMANCE
STANINE 3

Students in stanine 3 also most often score in the minimal performance category on criterion measures. Stanine 3 is equivalent to percentiles 11th–22nd. General characteristics and needs of this subgroup include the following:

- Usually can read and perform math on a low level
- May require special services, depending upon further evaluation
- Need some very targeted assistance in basic reading and math
- Can profit from additional time in reading and math class
- Need to be engaged with new material rather than having to repeat regular class work
- Can justifiably expect their test scores to improve somewhat with effort

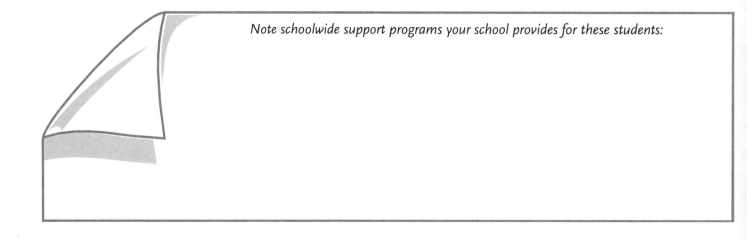

Note schoolwide support programs your school provides for these students:

SLIGHTLY BELOW-AVERAGE PERFORMANCE
STANINE 4

Students in stanine 4 also most often score in the basic performance category on criterion measures. Stanine 4 is equivalent to percentiles 23rd–39th.

This group of students, because they represent a sizable percentage of an average distribution, can have the most profound effect on group averages that are used in many accountability systems. General characteristics and needs of the stanine 4 subgroup include the following:

- Are most often very capable learners
- Can be relied upon to improve their performance with a limited amount of instructional intervention
- Usually have gaps in their knowledge base, lack organizational skills, or have learning differences that are not severe
- Are particularly suited to instructional interventions such as tutoring programs, learn-to-learn instruction, and academic mentors
- Do well in learning environments that recognize and reward individual growth

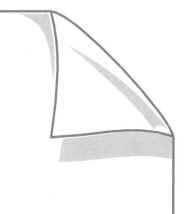

Note schoolwide support programs your school provides for these students:

AVERAGE TO SLIGHTLY ABOVE-AVERAGE PERFORMANCE
STANINES 5 & 6

Students in stanines 5 & 6 also most often score in either the basic or mastery performance categories on criterion measures.

Stanine 5 is equivalent to percentiles 40th–59th and stanine 6 is equivalent to percentiles 60th–76th. General characteristics of these groups include the following:

- Can profit from learn-to-learn instruction, tutoring, and mentor support
- Benefit by working in heterogeneous learning groups
- Often goal directed and profit from knowing (1) exactly where they are with respect to their comparative performance on academic measures and (2) specifically what they need to do to improve
- Can be very motivated to improve their academic performance in challenging learning environments

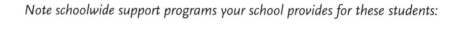

Note schoolwide support programs your school provides for these students:

WELL ABOVE-AVERAGE PERFORMANCE
STANINES 7 & 8

Students in stanines 7 & 8 also most often score in the mastery or above-average categories on criterion measures.

These students are rarely included in supplemental learning programs. Their performance ranges from the 77th through the 95th national percentile. General characteristics and needs of this subgroup include the following:

- Often forgotten because they are expected to do well
- Prosper when they know what is expected of them
- Enjoy going beyond the basic acquisition of the material to devise creative ways to challenge ideas
- Require recognition for their accomplishments
- Best suited as peer tutors to the lower subgroups
- Often have undetected problems gaining acceptance from other students and should be reviewed regularly by counseling staff

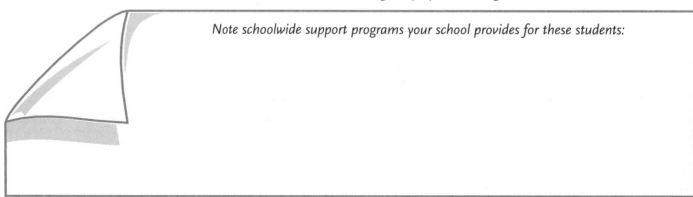

Note schoolwide support programs your school provides for these students:

SUPERIOR PERFORMANCE
STANINE 9

Students in stanine 9 can also be predicted to score in the highest performance category on criterion measures.

The 9th stanine includes students who score in the top 4% of all students tested. General characteristics and needs of this subgroup include the following:

- Most often highly motivated learners
- Unlikely that they can raise their performance much (in most circumstances)
- Can be taught to be peer tutors and benefit greatly from working with other less-able students
- Benefit from greater challenges, especially when those challenges are at the very high end of the complexity scale
- Should be reviewed for advanced placement and/or gifted programs
- Often have difficulty gaining acceptance from other students and should be reviewed regularly by counseling staff

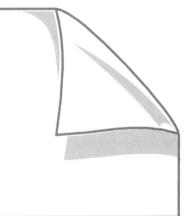

Note schoolwide support programs your school provides for these students:

The stanine characteristics listed above represent general descriptions of learners and should be validated by teacher judgment. Moreover, stanines should never be used to create permanent instructional groups. Rather they can best be used as a guide for identifying and working appropriately with all learners.

CRITERION-REFERENCED PERFORMANCE

Criterion-referenced test scores are very different from norm-referenced test scores. Criterion-referenced tests do not measure growth per se, nor do they draw particular attention to student-to-student comparisons on academic measures. Rather, they are designed to determine mastery in a specific content domain or minimum competency. The underlying assumption of criterion-referenced testing is that testing should be aligned to what is taught and that every child, given the appropriate instruction, support, and resources should achieve, at least, a minimal passing score. In reality, however, many students do not achieve minimal scores, and the alignment between what is taught and what is tested is particularly suspect.

When teachers use criterion-referenced data to help students who have failed to meet the minimal standard, they need to know the following:

1. *What proportion of items that measure prerequisite levels of knowledge and abilities did a student answer correctly?*

2. *What proportion of items that measure on-level knowledge and abilities did a student answer correctly?*

For example, the following sixth-grade mathematics expectations were published to help teachers prepare students for a criterion-referenced test: Factor whole numbers into primes, read and write numerals for decimals through ten-thousandths, mentally multiply and divide powers of ten, use models to explain concepts or solve problems involving ratio, proportion, and percent with whole numbers. Obviously, these expectations vary greatly in terms of cognitive difficulty as well as when they are taught during sixth grade. Missing is any information teachers can use to define test items that will deal with what sixth graders should be expected to know upon entering sixth grade and what they should learn during sixth grade and the order in which these concepts should be learned.

Having information that identifies the items a student answered incorrectly at the prerequisite level and at the on-level level of performance clearly profiles an individual student's knowledge, skills, and ability in ways that indicate which skills must be supported immediately and which should be supported in the future. These profiles are also useful for grouping students in classrooms and reporting to parents about the specific content a student must master to be successful.

This process of converting existing standardized test data into information teachers and students can use to guide student learning links test data to teaching and learning processes in several ways: (1) it takes the mystery out of what constitutes improvement on high-stakes tests; (2) it draws attention to the needs of the learner and informs decisions about school-sponsored learning support activities; and (3) it increases the capacity of teachers to provide parents with diagnostic information about what they can do to help their children succeed in school.

FRAMING SUCCESS

School improvement is about changing the contexts of schooling to guarantee that more students experience learning success. Standardized test results used appropriately can reveal the following:

1. The names and numbers of students who are growing at an appropriate rate as evidenced by the fact that they have met or exceeded their academic growth targets for this school year or have achieved appropriate levels of mastery on criterion measures.

2. The names and numbers of students who are not growing as evidenced by the fact that they have not met their academic growth targets for this school year or have not achieved appropriate levels of mastery on criterion measures.

3. The names and numbers of students who improved their performance as a result of schoolwide instructional support programs.

These names and numbers are fundamental to the school improvement process. What matters is to have schoolwide systems in place that support classroom teaching and learning. The goal is to guarantee not one student "falls through the cracks" and all students the opportunity to learn in a school that helps them focus attention and energy on becoming an effortful learner, no matter what their circumstances are.

Once students see for themselves that gains in performance are possible, however modest, they begin to connect learning and success. A school that keeps high-, average-, and low-performing students growing toward increasingly complex levels of learning is a school that is improving. The goal is to guarantee that not one student falls through the cracks because the school helps all students focus attention and energy on learning, no matter what the learner's circumstances.

It is not unreasonable to envision the future development of a new breed of standardized tests, tests that measure and report what teachers need to know to improve the context of learning for all students. Perhaps Edward Tenner is correct that "sometimes things can go right only by first going very wrong."

Test data used appropriately in school improvement projects can be linked to learning in several ways as follows:

- To provide general feedback to students on academic progress
- To screen students for special programs
- To inform parents of student performance
- To inform teacher judgments about improving classroom instruction
- To organize schoolwide learning support programs that make sure no student falls through the cracks
- To validate student and teacher efforts to improve
- To guide professional development activities
- To gauge program strengths and identify opportunities for program improvements
- To promote public accountability
- To monitor continuous progress.

TAKING ACTION

Action Items: Linking Testing to Teaching and Learning
Review the following suggestions for improving student academic performance. Which of these are presently used in your schoolwide instructional assistance programs? What additional programs or strategies could help your school attain its academic goals?

TAKING ACTION

USING ASSESSMENT DATA TO HELP STUDENTS TO MONITOR THEIR OWN PROGRESS IS BEST PRACTICE IN TEACHING.

ALL STUDENTS

SUGGESTED

- *Adviser/advisee conferences to interpret test data and set learning goals*

- *Parent test-interpretation seminars*

- *Newsletters explaining test improvement strategies*

- *Rewards and recognition programs for year-to-year student gains in academic performance*

- *Subject-area study guides and planners*

ACTION STATEMENTS: ALL STUDENTS

We will:

VERY LOW PERFORMANCE GROUPS (STANINES 1 & 2)

SUGGESTED

- Screening for special services

- Concentrated reading support programs

- Basic math tutoring programs

- Technology support for challenging low-performance learners

- Academic counseling groups

- Alternative testing programs online

- Opportunities to learn with average and above average students

- High-interest projects

ACTION ITEM: STANINES 1 & 2

We will:

WELL BELOW-AVERAGE PERFORMANCE GROUPS (STANINE 3)

SUGGESTED

- *Extended reading and language instruction*

- *Extended math instruction when warranted*

- *Home resource packets*

- *Learning partners programs*

- *Classroom grouping by interest*

- *Periodic assessment of performance*

ACTION ITEM: STANINE 3

We will:

SLIGHTLY BELOW-AVERAGE PERFORMANCE GROUPS (STANINE 4)

SUGGESTED

- *Homework help programs*

- *Formal subject-area tutorial programs*

- *Supervised study hall*

- *Learn-to-learn instruction and support materials*

- *Classroom grouping by mixed ability*

- *Technology support for guided practice*

ACTION ITEM: STANINE 4

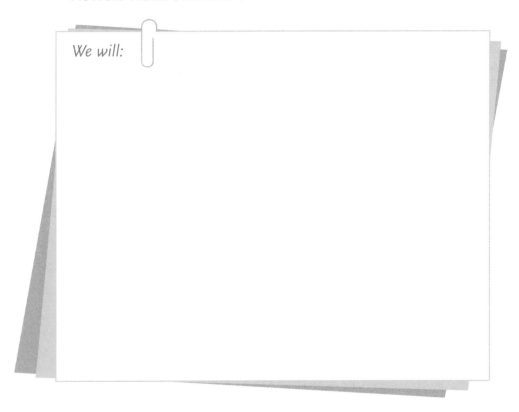

We will:

AVERAGE TO ABOVE-AVERAGE PERFORMANCE GROUPS (STANINES 5 & 6)

SUGGESTED

- *Accelerated learning programs*

- *High-challenge schoolwide academic projects*

- *Opportunities to work with advanced learners*

- *Opportunities to serve as academic mentors for younger students*

- *Increased demands for research beyond the textbook*

- *Flexible learning groups (interest, mixed, and by performance)*

- *Explicit information on the requisites of exemplary performance*

- *Opportunities to work with all other performance groups*

ACTION ITEM: STANINES 5 & 6

We will:

WELL ABOVE-AVERAGE PERFORMANCE GROUPS (STANINES 7—9)

SUGGESTED

- Compacting programs

- Counselor watch programs

- Opportunities to tutor other students

- Increased demands for research beyond the textbook

- Evaluation for gifted programs

- Explicit information on the requisites of exemplary performance

- Opportunities to work with all other performance groups

ACTION ITEM: STANINES 7—9

We will:

A CAUTIONARY NOTE

James Popham has written extensively on the limitations of standardized achievement tests as expected outcomes of schooling. He cites three reasons why standardized tests, as they are presently designed, poorly represent the real impact of teachers and schools on learners.

FIRST,

scores on nationally constructed standardized tests are greatly influenced by a student's aptitude or socioeconomic status (SES). In a recent review of prominent, nationally constructed standardized tests, Popham found that 50% of the variance in reading subtest items and 75% of variance in language arts subtest items were either aptitude or SES linked. This means that schools with a large number of students from lower-income families will fare poorly when compared to schools serving more affluent students.

SECOND,

because the modern curriculum is largely driven by mandated content standards that vary greatly from state to state, a reasonable match between what students are taught and what is tested on nationally produced criterion-referenced standardized tests is extremely difficult to achieve. These tests sample only a small percentage of the content standards teachers must teach in a given school year.

THIRD,

and perhaps most troublesome, all norm-referenced standardized achievement tests and more recently developed criterion-referenced tests select test items that discriminate between high-scoring students and low-scoring students. Thus, test items answered correctly by no more than half of the students tested are preferred to items answered correctly by too many students. Selecting test items that differentiate between high- and low-scoring students is also what makes them absurd as indicators of the degree to which schools are reducing the "gaps" between high- and low-performing groups of students.

Teachers need to help parents and students understand that standardized tests are quite different from other forms of academic assessment. Unlike exams, observations, examining student work or teacher-made tests, standardized tests produce very stable, consistent results. On standardized tests, student scores do not change drastically over the years of schooling. For many students, especially those in the average and below-average performance categories, catching up with high-achieving students is not a realistic goal.

MAKING SENSE

THE VOCABULARY OF TEST PERFORMANCE

ADVISER/ADVISEE PROGRAMS

are periodically scheduled meetings between a student and a faculty adviser to interpret test data, set academic growth targets, and provide guidance and support for student learning throughout the school year.

AGGREGATE DATA

is a term that refers to the practice of taking a set of scores into account as a whole. For example, the third-grade reading score is an aggregate score that references all third-grade reading scores using a measure of central tendency to define the whole. At the school level, a score that is closer to the source, for example, Harold Jackson's third-grade reading score, is preferred for instructional decisions.

ALTERNATIVE TESTING PROGRAMS

are off-level testing programs designed to provide regular feedback for students who are performing in the lowest-performance categories.

ASSESSMENT LITERACY

is the capacity to examine student performance data and make critical sense of it. Using this understanding, educators can make changes needed to increase student success. Above all, it involves engaging teachers and students together in shaping ongoing learning for greater improvement.

BENCHMARKS

are translations of content standards into specific statements of knowledge, products, skills, and/or understanding that students should attain as a result of instruction.

COMPACTING PROGRAMS

are opportunities for advanced students to provide evidence that they have completed in advance all requirements for a unit of instruction. Once demonstrated, these students are given freedom to work with another student, conduct research of interest, use a technology to advance their understanding of the subject, or engage in a learning task approved by the teacher.

COMPOSITE SCORE

is a norm-referenced score that represents the total score for the entire test battery. Because the composite score is an aggregate of all subtests, it is intended for use as a general indicator of student performance.

CONCENTRATED READING SUPPORT

is the allocation of additional time for low-performing students to work with a qualified reading instructor.

COUNSELOR WATCH PROGRAMS

are student-performance monitoring programs that guarantee that high-performing students, students who often go unnoticed until they fail, receive timely support for personal and academic problems.

CORE TOTAL

is a norm-referenced score that represents a composite of the total reading, total language, and total math scores. The Core Total, or on some standardized tests the Total Score, is a useful representation of basic literacy and can be used to chart student growth from year to year.

CRITERION-REFERENCED TESTS (CRTs)

are standardized achievement measures that measure student performance against predetermined criteria that are established prior to testing. Criterion-referenced tests cover a specific content domain and are used to determine if a student or group of students have gained an agreed-upon level of proficiency with respect to that content domain. In this way, CRTs measure performance with regard to a particular standard. On criterion-referenced tests, achievement is assessed relative to the test itself and the level of mastery of the instructional objectives that gave rise to the test.

DEVELOPMENTAL STANDARD SCORE

is an equal interval scale of scores that is continuous from kindergarten to grade 12. This scale is the norm-referenced scale most suitable for determining student achievement growth from year to year. Developmental Standard Scores are derived for grade-equivalent comparisons. The Median (Md) Standard Score for each grade reflects typical student performance in that grade.

DISAGGREGATED DATA

is the practice of separating testing results to isolate variations among different subgroups of students. Used traditionally, disaggregated statistics inform judgments about how well specific gender, ethnic, or performance groups are performing. Disaggregated data helps educators isolate problems and root causes of performance problems.

EQUAL INTERVAL SCALES

are most appropriate for use in calculating annual student growth. Those statistics that have the same meaning throughout their whole range of values are know as equal interval statistics.

EXTENDED MATH INSTRUCTION

is a double block of math instruction for students who are well-below average yet do not qualify for special services. Research supports that with additional instruction these students can be expected to actively participate during regular math instruction and over time improve their math ability. Double-block instruction need not be scheduled consecutively.

EXTENDED READING INSTRUCTION

is a double block of reading instruction for students who are well-below average and yet do not qualify for special services. Research supports that with additional instruction these students can be expected to actively participate during regular classes and over time improve their overall academic ability. Double-block instruction need not be scheduled consecutively.

FLEXIBLE INSTRUCTIONAL GROUPING

is the practice of grouping students for instruction using interest, mixed performance, or cognitive complexity as the criteria for selecting members of the group. Groups should be rotated using these criteria throughout the year.

FORMATIVE ASSESSMENTS

are assessments of student performance that provide timely, contextualized feedback that is useful for helping teachers and students during the learning process. Formative assessments are particularly effective for students who have not done well in school.

HIGH-CHALLENGE PROJECTS

are academic projects that require the student to conduct considerable research beyond the textbook for their completion.

HOME RESOURCE PACKETS

are learning materials designed to help low-performing students work with parents or guardians at home to reinforce basic concepts.

HOMEWORK ASSISTANCE PROGRAMS

are before- and afterschool programs designed to provide a supportive environment for slightly below-average and average students to work with a teacher, student tutor, or parent volunteer to complete classroom assignments.

INSTRUCTIONALLY SUPPORTIVE ACHIEVEMENT TESTS

are large-scale achievement tests that provide score-based accountability information needed to evaluate the quality of a school and also help teachers do a better job of teaching their students.

LEARN-TO-LEARN INSTRUCTION

considered by many researchers as the most prominent cause of underperformance in school, provides poorly organized or uninformed students with efficient strategies for learning effectively in formal learning environments.

LONGITUDINAL DATA

is concerned with the development of students over time. Instead of a snapshot of student performance on one test, longitudinal data, usually at least three years, yields a more reliable profile of the learner.

MENTOR PROGRAMS

are learning support programs that pair a high-performing student with a less-able one for the purpose of supporting learning.

NATIONAL PERCENTILE RANK

is a norm-referenced scale used to rank a student's performance as compared to similar students. The National Percentile Rank indicates the percentage of other students who scored below the student. If a student scored in the 68th percentile, she scored better than 68% of the students in the norm group. Percentiles, because the distance between them is not represented as equal interval statistics, should never be added, subtracted, or averaged.

NORMAL CURVE EQUIVALENT (NCE)

is a norm-referenced scale used to compare relative performance on different tests. The Normal Curve Equivalent divides the normal population into 99 units. NCEs are especially useful for comparing relative performance on different tests. For example, if a student's NCE for vocabulary was 36 and for math concepts was 52, it could be said that this student was significantly stronger in math than vocabulary.

NORM-REFERENCED TESTS (NRTs)

are standardized tests that compare one student's performance to a group of other students used as the "norm." Norm-referenced tests are given to a large representative sample of students and norms or standards of performance are established. Other students' scores are then measured against the standard. Unlike criterion-referenced tests, norm-referenced tests do not establish a level of proficiency, but rather report a student's performance compared to other similar students.

PARENT TESTING SEMINAR

is a teacher-led seminar designed to help parents interpret and understand standardized test data. These seminars are usually held at the beginning of the school year.

RAW SCORE

is the number of items answered correctly. For example, if a test has 50 items and a student gets 28 items correct, the raw score would be 28.

REAGGREGATE

is a term used here to describe the practice of reconfiguring standardized testing data in ways that give evidence of schooling effects that were not obvious in other forms of reporting.

RELIABILITY

is a test to see whether scores from a test are consistent. If there are two versions of a test, performance on either test should be similar.

REWARDS AND RECOGNITION PROGRAMS

are motivational programs designed to affirm and reward student efforts to improve academic performance over one year of schooling. Rewards programs utilize affiliation products such as T-shirts, baseball caps, banners, and flags containing school logos.

SCREENING FOR SPECIAL SERVICES

is the practice of using standardized test data to determine placement of students in special classes for gifted or special need.

STANINE

is a standard score system that divides the normal population on a nine-unit scale (standard-nine). Stanines indicate a student's relative standing within a normal group. The stanine is the most appropriate normed scale for determining individual or group strengths and weaknesses in content areas.

SUMMATIVE ASSESSMENTS

are evaluations of student achievement that summarize a student's performance at a particular point in time, say at the end of a school year or course. Summative assessments provide information that teachers can use to organize their teaching. However, research cautions that summative assessments tend to have a negative effect upon student learning.

TECHNOLOGY SUPPORT

is now abundantly available to support learning and test performance. These products have been shown to help motivate students and provide periodic opportunities for students to self-test themselves and reinforce what they are learning.

TUTORIAL PROGRAMS

are regularly scheduled meetings between a caring, informed adult and a student needing academic support.

VALIDITY

is an internal test to see if a standardized test actually measures what it is supposed to measure.

LOOKING WIDER

SUGGESTED READINGS

Black, P., Harrison, C., Lee, C., Marshall, B., and Wiliam, D., "Working Inside the Black Box: Assessment for Learning in the Classroom," *in* Phi Delta Kappan, *September 2004, pp. 9-21*

Danielson, Charlotte, "Enhancing Student Achievement," Association for Supervision and Curriculum Development, 2002

Hart, Betty, and Risley, Todd R., "Meaningful Differences," Paul H. Brookes Publishing Co., 1995

Popham, W. James, "The Truth About Testing," Association for Supervision and Curriculum Development, 2001

Stiggins, Rick, "New Assessment Beliefs for a New School Mission," *in* Phi Delta Kappan, *September 2004, pp. 22-27*

Tenner, Edward, "Why Things Bite Back: Technology and the Revenge of Unintended Consequences," Alfred A. Knopf, Inc., 1996

Thorndike, Robert M., "Measurement and Evaluation in Psychology and Education," Sixth Edition, Prentice Hall, Inc., 1997

White, Stephen, "Show Me the Proof: Tools and Strategies to Make Data Work for You," Advanced Learning Press, 2005

SIGNS OF SUCCESS WORTH FIGHTING FOR

- *Parents, students, and teachers who can make critical sense of test data*
- *Test data used to inform teaching practices*
- *Reading and basic support programs for low-performing students*
- *Achievement recognition for all students working to their capacity*
- *Study skills instruction for underachievers*
- *Extensive use of formative and performance assessments*

INDICATORS OF STUDENT LEARNING SUCCESS

INDICATORS	EXPECTATIONS
Grade Distribution	
NRT Results	
CRT Results	
Standards-Based Performance Assessments	
Formative Assessments	
Student Accomplishments Beyond the School	
Other	

CREATING A LEARNING PLACE

PERSONAL REFLECTIONS:

Jot down your main learnings from Chapter 3

CHAPTER FOUR: PROMOTING PURPOSE AND COMMUNITY

ESSENTIAL QUESTION:

What can we do to guarantee that not one student misses the message that we are all here to support and affirm their growth and development?

BIG IDEA — PROMOTING A SENSE OF PURPOSE AND COMMUNITY IS EVERYBODY'S JOB.

What lies behind us and what lies ahead of us are insignificant compared to what lies within us.

—Oliver Wendell Holmes

Schools promote a sense of purpose by providing opportunities for students to translate the values of the school community into personal behaviors. Schools that reach more learners do so by becoming more coherent and consistent in their approach to communicating their values. Creating infrastructures that link the daily context of the school to values like effort, cooperation, and recognition is the key. This means creating a safe umbrella for all types of learners to feel welcome and affirmed, refusing to let even one student miss the message, and helping learners believe in their own potential for growth. A sense of purpose gives meaning to the school program and is yet another context variable that is within the school's power to change for the better.

GETTING STARTED

GETTING STARTED

What personal learner behaviors does our school value? Describe a model student here.

How does our school model and teach respect for others?

> One looks back with appreciation to the brilliant teachers, but with gratitude to those who touched our human feelings. The curriculum is so much necessary raw material, but warmth is the vital element for the growing plant and for the soul of the child.
>
> —Carl Jung

LOOKING DEEPER

WHAT DO YOU SEE IN A SCHOOL WHERE SENSE OF PURPOSE AND COMMUNITY IS PROMOTED?

Place a check indicating an aspect of your school program that is particularly effective.

MORAL PURPOSE WRIT LOUD

__ Displayed codes of conduct with emphasis on principled behavior

__ Displayed core value statements (what we stand for)

__ Displayed mission statement

__ High levels of professional efficacy evidenced in teacher behaviors

__ Modeled commitments for social justice

__ Well-publicized school honor codes

__ Other (describe)

Notes:

Discuss evidence of your assessment.

TRADITIONS OF RESPECT

___ Collegiality and trust modeled publicly

___ Frequent respectful exchanges between teachers and students (good morning/thank you/can I help you/how are you?)

___ Frequently expressed appreciation for acts of kindness

___ Posted inspirational sayings

___ Regular communication about principled behavior with students and parents

___ Regular school meetings and convocations about modeling respectful behavior

___ Student behavior codes that personalize respectful behavior

___ Student-generated service projects

___ Tangible reinforcement of evidence of respect

___ Other (describe)

Notes:

Discuss evidence of your assessment.

CULTURAL AND PHYSICAL CONTEXTS

___ Advocacy counseling programs

___ Affiliation artifacts (hats/shirts/badges/banners)

___ Art projects displayed throughout the school

___ Big brothers and big sisters programs

___ Career day programs

___ Celebrations and regular rituals

___ Common meeting places

___ Cultural arts program offerings

___ Dress-up days

___ Enthusiastic and optimistic staff gatherings

___ Frequent laughter and joy for learning

___ Hallway bulletin boards that reinforce the value of respect and teamwork

___ Laughter and smiles

___ Music programs

___ Plants, trees, and gardens

___ Positive symbols

___ Safe and clean classrooms and restrooms

___ School banners

___ Subject-area clubs

___ T-shirt days

___ Visually pleasing hallways and classrooms

___ Other (describe)

Notes:

Discuss evidence of your assessment.

SCHOOLWIDE MOTIVATION

__ Academic achievement awards
__ Arts recognition
__ Athletic recognition
__ Attendance awards
__ Citizenship and service awards
__ Current examples of model student work throughout the school
__ Displayed honor rolls
__ Evidence of service projects
__ Music recognition
__ Orientation programs for new students
__ Public recognition of student effort
__ Recognition for academic excellence
__ Regular student adviser/advisee conferences
__ School spirit events
__ Service awards
__ Student and teacher smiles and laughter
__ Student-led report card conferences
__ Subject-area recognition
__ Welcome kits for teachers and students
__ Other (describe)

Notes:

Discuss evidence of your assessment.

COMMUNITY LINKS

__ Incremental academic goals for all students given to parents
__ Informal teacher/parent communications
__ Parent breakfast meetings
__ Parent literacy program
__ Parent newsletters
__ Parent tutors
__ Regular parent notifications of student progress
__ Solicitation of parents as resources
__ Student engaged in community publications
__ Student engaged in creating and explaining academic projects to visitors
__ Student engaged in teaching the use of instructional resources
__ Student helping with goal setting
__ Visible evidence that parents are welcome in the school
__ Visitor orientation packets available
__ Other (describe)

Notes:

Discuss evidence of your assessment.

It is one of the most beautiful compensations of this life that no man can sincerely try to help another without helping himself.

—Ralph Waldo Emerson

LOOKING FOR EVIDENCE

THAT YOUR SCHOOL IS PROMOTING A SENSE OF PURPOSE AND COMMUNITY

Using the descriptors listed on pages 72 to 74, on a scale of 1–10, how does your school rate as a place where promoting a sense of purpose and community exists? Explain your assessment.

1	2	3	4	5	6	7	8	9	10

SUPPORT YOUR ASSESSMENT

TAKING ACTION

PART 1: 360° FEEDBACK ACTIVITY

Directions: Use the 360° Feedback Template to interview anyone who has a connection to the school. Ask them what they like about the school and take notes on the graphic organizer provided. Share your findings and come to some agreement on what you have learned about how others "see" the school. Also determine what can be done to further guarantee deep and purposeful affiliations between teachers, students, parents, and administrators.

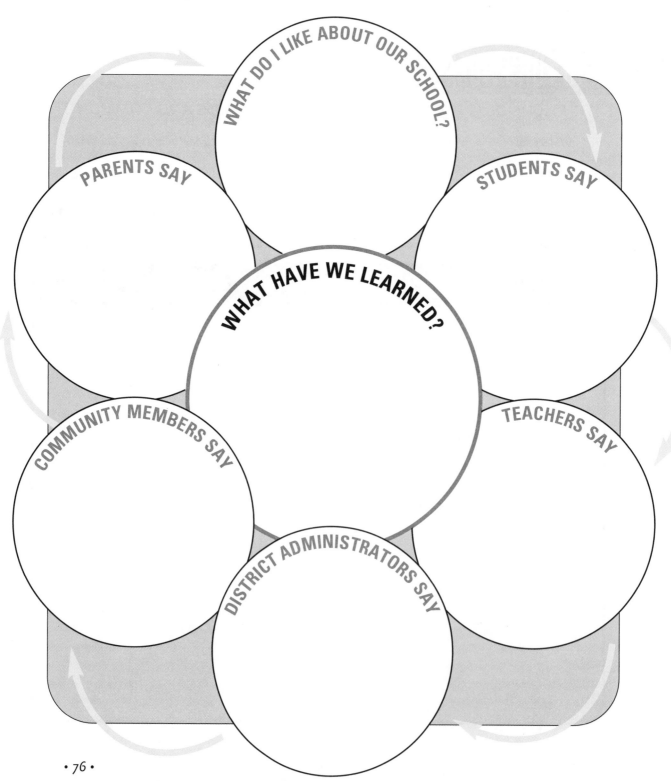

WHAT DO I LIKE ABOUT OUR SCHOOL?

PARENTS SAY

STUDENTS SAY

WHAT HAVE WE LEARNED?

COMMUNITY MEMBERS SAY

TEACHERS SAY

DISTRICT ADMINISTRATORS SAY

PART 2: ORGANIZE A FACULTY ACTION TEAM THAT WILL:

- *Create and display at least three posters that communicate a shared commitment to treat each other with respect.*

- *Review all discipline handbooks and policy manuals. Do these materials contain components that reinforce respectful, learning-oriented exchanges between teachers, students, parents, and administrators?*

- *Work together to introduce additional school routines and traditions aimed at and celebrating student, faculty, or community success.*

A good school for me is a place where everyone is teaching and everyone is learning—simultaneously under the same roof.

— Roland Barth

MAKING SENSE

THE VOCABULARY OF MORAL PURPOSE

AFFILIATION ARTIFACTS

are products that are used to build a sense of family in the school community and show affiliation and allegiance to an individual school. Examples of artifacts are student- and teacher-designed T-shirts, baseball caps, auto stickers, banners, rings, pendants, pins, etc.

BIG BROTHERS AND BIG SISTERS PROGRAMS

are student mentor programs that pair older boys and girls with younger students in an effort to provide ongoing support for the younger student and an opportunity to build character for the older students.

Living up to basic ethical standards in the classroom – discipline, tolerance, honesty – is one of the most important ways children learn how to function in society at large.

—Eloise Salholz

CODE OF CONDUCT

is a published agreement describing a group commitment to act responsibly and treat others with respect.

COLLEGIALITY

is shared power and authority vested among people of goodwill. In schools collegiality is demonstrated by a willingness to listen to the ideas of others and help each other by working as a contributing member of a team dedicated to a shared purpose. In schools where collegiality is strong, everyone is a part of the solution.

COMMON MEETING PLACES

are spaces allocated for groups to gather to meet socially or do work for the school.

CORE VALUE STATEMENT

is a published statement describing how the school adds value to the lives of all members of its community.

EFFICACY

is the power and efficiency to produce a desired effect. In schools, efficacy is used to describe individual teacher beliefs that confirm that quality-schooling practices have real and lasting effects upon learners.

PRINCIPLED BEHAVIOR

is behavior guided by principles of fairness, trust, honesty, fellowship, and respect for the dignity of everyone.

POSITIVE SYMBOLS

are inspirational sayings, guides for appropriate action, motivational advice, mascots, school banners, logos, school spirit ribbons, and flags.

REGULAR RITUALS

are scheduled events that draw attention to deeply held values. Rituals communicate what's important in schools.

SERVICE AWARDS

are awards given to students for their participation in school and community projects that provide service to those in need.

TANGIBLE SUPPORT

is extending yourself to help others with time and material as well as human resources. It is sustained by the belief that one's colleagues are doing the same.

TRUST BUILDING

is reliance on the character, integrity, or ability of a person or thing. In schools trust is cultivated by making a personal commitment to do everything we can to add to the common good of the school. The well-being of a school can be judged by the number of secrets it keeps. Trust does not exist in the same place with secrets.

WALK-THRU

Observe your school in action. Note indicators that provide evidence for a Sense of Purpose and Community. Select those indicators and create a Schoolwide Walk-Thru form so as to focus attention and to reinforce your school's accomplishments in this area.

This visual representation will help make your school's existing potential both public and visible. It will also create new energy needed to move to action.

SCHOOLWIDE WALK-THRU

☐ VISITING TEACHER
☐ ADMINISTRATOR
☐ OTHER _____

SCHOOL _____

_____

DATE _____

SIGNED _____

Promoting Purpose and Community

- Displayed Code of Conduct
- Displayed Mission Statement
- Published Honor Code

Promoting Purpose and Community

- Modeled Respectful Behavior
- Academic Achievement Recognition
- Displayed Honor Rules

Promoting Purpose and Community

- Citizenship Awards
- Service Projects
- School Spirit Events

LOOKING WIDER

SUGGESTED READINGS

Barth, Roland S., "Improving Schools from Within," Jossey-Bass Publishers, 1990

Block, Peter, "Stewardship," Berrett-Koehler Publishers, 1993

Palmer, Parker J., "The Courage to Teach," Jossey-Bass Publishers, 1998

Peterson, Kent D. and Deal, Terrence E., "The Shaping School Culture Handbook," Jossey-Bass – A Wiley Company, 2002

Purkey, William Watson and Novak, John M., "Inviting School Success," Wadsworth Publishing Company, 1996

SIGNS OF SUCCESS WORTH FIGHTING FOR

- *Parents as learning partners*
- *Schooling practices that reinforce a culture of learning*
- *Regular use of school facilities by community groups*
- *Partnerships with business and community leaders*
- *Public recognition of student and teacher achievements*
- *Regularly published newsletter*
- *Smiles, laughter, and a calm purposeful atmosphere*

Good teaching cannot be reduced to technique: good teaching comes from the identity and integrity of the teacher.

—Parker Palmer

CREATING A LEARNING PLACE

PERSONAL REFLECTIONS:

Jot down your main learnings from Chapter 4

CHAPTER FIVE: MAKING LEARNING SUPPORT ACCESSIBLE

ESSENTIAL QUESTION:

What can we do to expand or refine our schoolwide academic support programs so as to reduce unnecessary barriers to learning success?

BIG IDEA — MAKING LEARNING ACCESSIBLE THROUGHOUT THE SCHOOL DAY AND BEYOND IS A MAJOR "GAP CLOSER."

Invited to use a variety of approaches to instruction, teachers in Learning Places stretch the limits of success by drawing students ever closer to personal learning success. They take seriously their obligation to link appropriate curriculum with the conditions of learning in ways that affirm learning success.

Day by day, what you choose, what you think, and what you do is what you become.

—Heraclitus

When learning is accessible, every student is challenged to succeed regardless of achievement level and no student falls through the cracks. Teachers define learning in terms of individual student growth rather than preestablished norms. Classrooms are characterized by high student engagement and challenging assignments.

When learning is accessible, average students have more opportunities for peer assistance. High achievers can select challenging coursework. Slower readers can take advantage of additional reading opportunities in areas of their interest. Students with poor work habits receive study skills instruction. Special needs students are expected to complete meaningful work. And all students are responsible for helping each other.

In Learning Places, student success is measured one student at a time using increased levels of learning performance as the yardstick.

Making learning highly accessible involves teachers holding themselves and each other accountable for creating enriched opportunities for learning. This means orchestrating the schoolwide contexts of learning to give meaning to the belief that in our school we expect every student and every teacher to succeed.

They also understand the importance of helping each and every student acquire a positive attitude toward learning. They teach students how to tackle new problems, how to take notes, how to study, how to manage time, and how to think insightfully. The school offers these same learning opportunities for teachers and other staff members.

GETTING STARTED

How does our school provide learning challenges beyond classroom work for high-ability students?

GETTING STARTED

What schoolwide programs support students who are failing?

GETTING STARTED

What is our school's response for average students who are underachievers?

GETTING STARTED

How are volunteer parents used to increase student access to learning?

LOOKING DEEPER

WHAT DO YOU SEE IN A SCHOOL WHERE LEARNING IS HIGHLY ACCESSIBLE?

Place a check indicating an aspect of your school program that is particularly effective. (See the Making Sense segment of this chapter for definitions of unfamiliar terms.)

SCHOOLWIDE LEARNING SUPPORT

__ Academic buzz in a hospitable atmosphere
__ Academic projects evidenced throughout the school
__ Access to honors curriculum
__ Adviser/Advisee conferences

__ Clearly articulated curriculum standards and benchmarks
__ Compacting options for highly effortful students
__ Cooperative learning projects

__ Emphasis on student thinking
__ Evidence of student projects
__ Evidence of student self-assessment practices
__ Experiential learning materials used in classrooms
__ Experimentation and hypothesizing by teachers and students
__ Extended time in reading and math for appropriate students

__ Faculty advocates
__ Flexible grouping practices used in classrooms

__ Guided study hall programs with teacher support

__ High-challenge courses and curriculum
__ High student engagement/challenging assignments

__ Highly visual three-dimensional representations of content displayed
__ Homework assistance programs before and after school
__ Homework huts, a quiet place to prepare for school

__ In-progress formal assessments of student work
__ Interactive teaching and active classrooms

__ Learning press (everything supports learning)
__ Learn-to-learn courses/programs

__ Peer tutors
__ Published course outlines and pacing guides

__ Reading instruction across content areas
__ Resources beyond the textbook available in all classrooms
__ Rubrics in use in classrooms

__ Schoolwide instructional support programs for average students
__ Schoolwide instructional support programs for high-performing students
__ Schoolwide instructional support programs for students with learning problems
__ Student academic contracts in use

__ Technology in use in classrooms

HIGHLIGHTING STRENGTH AND OPPORTUNITY IN SWOT

A SWOT analysis is a planning technique used primarily in business to determine an organization's capacity to meet its existing challenges. Review your work on Making Learning Accessible and meet with members of your study group to summarize your observations to date.

STRENGTHS
What are the key elements of our existing potential?

WEAKNESSES
What are our present limitations?

OPPORTUNITIES
What opportunities do we have to use our potential to achieve success?

THREATS
What factors are presently difficult to influence?

RUBRIC

ASSESSING EVIDENCE THAT YOUR SCHOOL IS MAKING LEARNING SUPPORT ACCESSIBLE TO ALL STUDENTS.

Directions: Using the information gathered thus far in this chapter, on a scale of 1–10, how does your school rate as a place that makes learning support accessible to all students? Explain.

SUPPORT YOUR ASSESSMENT

TAKING ACTION

Directions: Complete the following Task Planner and present your suggestions to the faculty at large.

MAKING LEARNING ACCESSIBLE

WHAT WORKS NOW:

PROPOSED ADDITIONS:

BARRIERS TO SUCCESS:

IMPLEMENTATION ACTION PLAN

FIRST:

THEN:

FINALLY:

TAKING ACTION

MAKING LEARNING ACCESSIBLE

GROUP ASSIGNMENTS:

1.

2.

3.

4.

MAKING SENSE

THE VOCABULARY OF LEARNING SUPPORT

COMPACTING PRACTICES

are classroom grouping strategies used to reward students who have demonstrated above-average performance or effort. At a designated time in a unit of instruction, students who have successfully completed their work and demonstrated understanding of the concepts taught are given choices of independent study, technology use, or working as mentors with other students. Compacting practices are not reserved for the brightest students; they are rewards for effort and evidence of learning in any student.

EXTENDED TIME IN READING AND MATH

are extended classes organized for students operating below the 4th stanine on standardized tests of performance in reading and math. These classes are linked to regular class work and are designed to provide additional processing time for completion of academic tasks.

FACULTY ADVISER

is a faculty member who meets regularly with a group of students to discuss their progress.

FLEXIBLE GROUPING

is a classroom grouping strategy that places students in learning groups based upon (1) interest, (2) a diversity of performance abilities and communication skills, and (3) ability to complete specific cognitive tasks. These groups are never permanent.

GUIDED STUDY HALLS

are scheduled opportunities for students to work with student mentors and teachers to further clarify and complete academic work.

HIGH-CHALLENGE COURSE OFFERINGS

are scheduled opportunities for students of all levels to qualify for coursework, study groups, or academic projects that involve completing learning tasks of higher complexity.

HOMEWORK HUTS

are designated areas where students can quietly prepare themselves for class, read, or study.

If you have the knowledge, let others light their candles by it.

——Thomas Fuller

INCREMENTAL PERFORMANCE TARGETS

are grade-level benchmarks for student performance written as rubrics that describe entry, on level, and advanced levels of performance.

IN-PROGRESS ASSESSMENTS

are interim reports depicting individual student progress toward standards and benchmarks written in both qualitative and narrative forms.

INTERACTIVE TEACHING

is an instructional strategy that focuses on high levels of student engagement and interaction with guided support from the teacher. It is not uncommon for students to assume the role of teacher during interactive learning segments.

LEARNING PRESS

is a term used to describe the practice of measuring every decision against its impact on student learning and time.

LEARN-TO-LEARN

is a learning strategy for personalizing, organizing, managing, and deepening understanding of material to be learned in formal learning settings.

LITERACY ACQUISITION PROFILES

are profiles designed by the faculty to clearly depict the acquisition of literary standards and benchmarks for performance. These profiles are used to motivate and inform student goal setting.

LONGITUDINAL DIAGNOSTIC DATA

is a three-year student profile highlighting individual student strengths, academic needs, and programs that target improving academic growth and capacity building.

The essence of our effort to see that every child has a chance must be to assure each an equal opportunity, not to become equal, but to become different—to realize whatever unique potential of body, mind and spirit he or she possesses.

—John Fischer

PACING GUIDES

are published course/unit descriptions with step-by-step timelines of learning tasks and expectations for performance.

READING ACROSS CONTENT AREAS

is the opportunity for students experiencing reading difficulty to have additional time during the school day to read with support in each discipline and especially disciplines that are of greatest interest to the student.

RUBRICS

are assessment tools that provide gradients of high to low in-progress feedback on individual student performance as compared to a standard for excellence.

SUBJECT MATTER UNIFIERS

are learn-to-learn strategies like previewing, note taking, mind mapping, visual time lines, prewriting templates, learning challenges, chapter tours, scaffolding summaries, graphic outlines, journals, word walls, learning logs, and content webs (see Studywhiz.com for examples).

TARGETED ACADEMIC INTERVENTION

is the practice of using academic interventions to make instruction more responsive to the academic needs of students. Examples of this form of intervention include the following: reading support classes, homework assistance programs, assignment to extended class time in reading and in math, study skills courses and learn-to-learn instruction, high-challenge projects and coursework, compacting opportunities, paired mentor programs, tutoring programs, adviser/advisee sessions, and counselors monitoring the progress of special needs learners.

WALK-THRU

is an informal observation tool used to collect specific examples of the contexts of teaching and learning. Walk-Thru data is used exclusively to inform and improve student learning; it is never used to evaluate a teacher or a school.

WALK-THRU

Observe your school in action. Note indicators that provide evidence for greater Access to Learning. Select those indicators and create a Schoolwide Walk-Thru form so as to focus attention and to reinforce your school's accomplishments in this area.

This visual representation will help make your school's existing potential both public and visible. It will also create new energy needed to move to action.

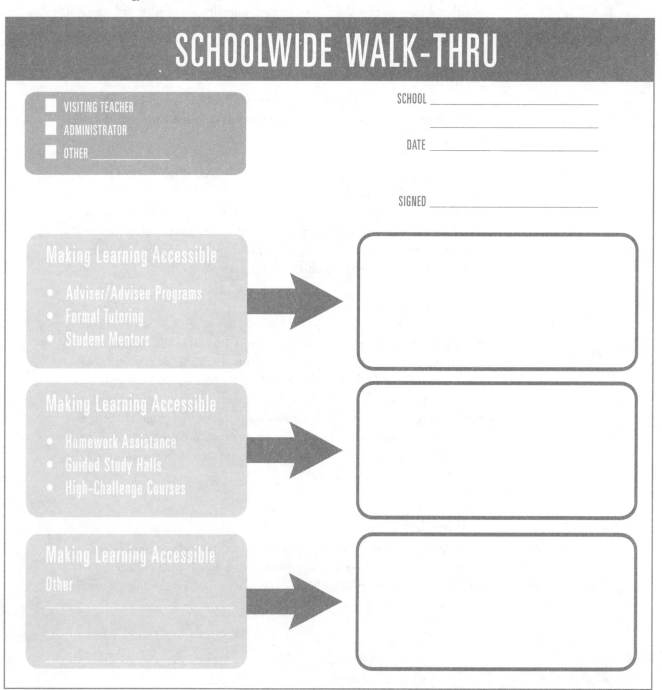

SCHOOLWIDE WALK-THRU

☐ VISITING TEACHER
☐ ADMINISTRATOR
☐ OTHER _____

SCHOOL _____

_____

DATE _____

SIGNED _____

Making Learning Accessible

- Adviser/Advisee Programs
- Formal Tutoring
- Student Mentors

Making Learning Accessible

- Homework Assistance
- Guided Study Halls
- High-Challenge Courses

Making Learning Accessible
Other

_____

_____

_____

LOOKING WIDER

SUGGESTED READINGS

Block, Cathy Collins, "Teaching Comprehension," Pearson Education, Inc., 2004

Caine, Renate Nummela, and Caine, Geoffrey, "Education on the Edge of Possibility," Association for Supervision and Curriculum Development, 1997

Darling-Hammond, Linda, "The Right to Learn," A Blueprint for Creating Schools That Work," Jossey-Bass, 2001

Flippo, Rona F., "Texts and Tests," Heinemann, 2004

Littky, Dennis, "The Big Picture," Association for Supervision and Curriculum Development, 2004

Novak, Joseph D., and Gowin, Bob, "Learning How to Learn," Cambridge University Press, 1984

Robinson, Adam, "What Smart Students Know," Crown Publishers, Inc., 1993

Springer, Marilee, "Learning and Memory," Association for Supervision and Curriculum Development, 1999

St. Germain, Clif, "StudyWhiz: A Guide to Better Grades," Pivot Point International, Inc., 2000

Tovani, Cris, "I Read It, But I Don't Get It," Stenhouse Publishers, 2000

SIGNS OF SUCCESS WORTH FIGHTING FOR

- *Students helping each other learn*
- *A school philosophy that encourages multiple attempts to learn*
- *Guided study halls and homework help sessions*
- *A fully integrated schoolwide instructional support program*
- *Frequent rewards for student effort*

> *A major part of the meaning of life is contained in the very process of discovering it.*
>
> —Ira Progoff

CREATING A LEARNING PLACE

PERSONAL REFLECTIONS:

Jot down your main learnings from Chapter 5

CHAPTER SIX: SHARING IDEAS ABOUT IMPROVING CLASSROOM TEACHING

ESSENTIAL QUESTION:

How can we guarantee that teachers search out, experiment with, guarantee and share ideas and resources for improving classroom teaching?

BIG IDEA — PROFESSIONAL RIGOR AND A PASSION FOR TEACHING ARE CONTAGIOUS.

An education that does not begin by evoking initiative and end by encouraging it must be wrong.

——Alfred North Whitehead

MINDSHIFT: *Active participation in the collective development of other teachers is a critical competency of modern teaching.*

In this Field Guide we have emphasized that personal collaboration and a focused sense of purpose amplify a school's influence on student learning. We have also suggested that by acting together to improve the contexts of the school at large, teachers, principals, parents, and students foster greater cohesion and shared commitment. Applying this cohesion and commitment to improve classroom teaching is the topic of Chapters 6 through 10.

As recent research confirms schools rarely improve one classroom at a time. Schools and classrooms improve collectively. Providing resources that simultaneously produce teacher and student development is yet another goal of this Field Guide.

Today, we know what good classroom teaching looks like. School effectiveness research in the 1970s and 1980s added to our understanding of the differences between effective and ineffective classrooms. Since then, educators have continued to test, refine, and publish these findings for use by classroom teachers. Among the most noteworthy of these publications is *Research You Can Use to Improve Results* (1999) by Kathleen Cotton. This compendium of effective schooling research provides a broad and integrated picture of schooling practices that can be used to stimulate discussions of instructional issues and guide school improvement initiatives.

MINDFUL TEACHING

Mindful Teaching is a framework for helping teachers incorporate knowledge about optimum conditions for learning into the day-to-day contexts of classrooms. Mindful Teaching is not a formula for teaching. Teaching is a growing living thing that evolves through years of searching and experimentation. Mindful Teaching is a set of core ideas that teachers can use to develop a personal philosophy for teaching that works best for their students. In this sense it is a road map with plenty of room for alternate routes.

Chapters 6 through 10 further expand the defining characteristics of Mindful Teaching as follows:

Personal participation is the universal principle of knowing.

—Michael Polanyi

FOUR PHASES OF MINDFUL TEACHING

1. READINESS

- Establish a reason/rationale for learning
- Connect to existing levels of student understanding
- Guide student curiosity and use exploratory discussion to build mutual respect
- Clarify misconceptions
- Explain expectations and schedules for new learning
- Provide a "road map" for new learning using visual advance organizers

2. DELIVERY

- Identify key concepts
- Systematically direct student attention to similarities and differences
- Define, explain, exchange, model, and relate important ideas
- Probe with questions and provide feedback
- Impose formal structure on material to be learned
- Guide student categorization/organization of ideas for future use

3. PERFORMANCE

- Demonstrate appropriate use and applications
- Guide student practice, challenge and construct applications of ideas
- Provide ongoing assessments, corrective feedback, and encouragement
- Engage students in experimentation, problem solving, and solution-finding activities

3. PERFORMANCE
(CONTINUED)

- Require and support student creation of learning products
- Build on student success and manage limitations
- Organize flexible learning groups

4. TRANSFER

- Facilitate multiple expressions/representations of subject matter learned
- Generate new questions and applications of ideas learned
- Guide student reflection and learning
- Help students consolidate and integrate new learning
- Move students to insightful thinking and writing
- Invite students to reflect on changes in their thinking as a result of new learning

GETTING STARTED

GETTING STARTED

What classroom practices make the biggest difference in student learning?

GETTING STARTED

What can teachers do to help each other teach more mindfully?

MAKING SENSE

PROFESSIONAL TEACHING COMMUNITY

is a teaching faculty that is organized around core elements of:

- Shared understanding and common values

- Collective inquiry

- Collaborative planning

- Action-oriented problem solving

- Shared responsibility

- Shared success

The law of nature is, Do the thing, and you shall have the power...

—Ralph Waldo Emerson

TAKING ACTION

*Authors Gerald Nadler and William Chandon have developed a **Smart Questions Approach (SQA)** to problem solving and creative solution finding that is particularly suited to getting people to openly share ideas and take action.*

Nadler and Chandon describe SQA as a process that blends people, purposes, solutions, and actions. What follows is an activity designed to use the SQA process to initiate inquiry and collaboration aimed at improving classroom teaching.

PROBLEM STATEMENT:

How can our school reduce teacher isolation and guarantee that teachers have opportunities to exchange ideas and resources on a daily basis?

DIRECTIONS: 1. Invite a group of teachers, an administrator, and a few interested parents to explore options for increasing teacher inquiry and collaboration into "best practices" in classroom teaching.

2. Plan several meetings to complete the questions in the **List-Organize-Decide (LOD)** matrix presented here. Please allow sufficient time between meetings for informal discussion, reflection, and refinement. Chapters 5 through 9 of this Field Guide provide substance for these initiatives.

3. Present your findings and recommendations to the school community for discussion, review, and recommendation.

NOTE WELL: *Competent, collegial teachers create exciting and engaging schools!*

PHASE ONE:

Getting people motivated and involved in a project is a difficult task.

LIST:

Generate a list of ideas that will reduce the isolation of teachers at your school.

ORGANIZE:

Organize your list into some type of pattern.

DECIDE:

Select appropriate options for getting teachers more involved in generating and sharing information about improving classroom teaching.

PHASE TWO:

What can we expect to change if we are successful?

LIST:

What are the immediate benefits to reducing teacher isolation?

ORGANIZE:

Organize your list into some type of pattern.

DECIDE:

Prioritize the benefits in terms of their immediate relevance to student learning.

PHASE THREE:

How can we survey and use what successful schools have done with regard to this problem?

LIST:
What have other schools done to reduce teacher isolation?

ORGANIZE:
Organize your list into some type of pattern.

DECIDE:
Prioritize promising options that can be implemented without additional staff or resources.

PHASE FOUR:

What can we do now?

LIST:
What specific strategies can we implement now to reduce teacher isolation and encourage the daily exchange of teaching strategies and resources?

ORGANIZE:
Organize your list into some type of pattern.

DECIDE:
Create an action plan for reducing teacher isolation.

LOOKING WIDER

SUGGESTED READINGS

Cotton, Kathleen, "Research You Can Use to Improve Results," Northwest Regional Educational Laboratory, ASCD, 2000

Curwin, Richard L., and Mendler, Allen N., "Discipline with Dignity," Association for Supervision and Curriculum Development, 1999

Friedman, Myles I., "Ensuring Student Success," The Institute for Evidence-Based Decision-Making in Education, Inc., 2000

Friedman, Myles I., and Fisher, Steven P., "Handbook on Effective Instructional Strategies," The Institute for Evidence-Based Decision-Making in Education, Inc., 1998

Lencioni, Patrick, "Overcoming the Five Dysfunctions of a Team," Jossey-Bass, Inc., 2005

Nadler, Gerald, and Chandon, William J., "Smart Questions," Jossey-Bass, Inc., 2004

Pfeffer, Jeffrey, and Sutton, Robert I., "The Knowing Doing Gap," Harvard Business School Publishing, 2000

Stronge, James H., "Qualities of Effective Teachers," Association for Supervision and Curriculum Development, 2002

Vaill, Peter B., "Learning as a Way of Being," Jossey-Bass, Inc., 1996

Zemelman, S., Daniels, H., and Hyde, A., "Best Practice," Heinemann, 1993

SIGNS OF SUCCESS WORTH FIGHTING FOR

- *Teachers helping each other*
- *Mini grants for innovative teaching*
- *Shared resources and teaching initiatives*
- *Interclassroom visitations and discussions of classroom teaching strategies that work*
- *Collaborative lesson planning*
- *Teaching mentors*

CREATING A LEARNING PLACE

PERSONAL REFLECTIONS:

Jot down your main learnings from Chapter 6

-
-
-
-
-

CHAPTER SEVEN: FOCUSING STUDENT INTEREST AND ATTENTION

ESSENTIAL QUESTION:

What can classroom teachers do, prior to formal instruction, to (1) communicate interest and enthusiasm for subject matter and (2) guarantee that students are prepared for learning success?

BIG IDEA — EFFECTIVE TEACHERS UNCOVER MATERIAL BEFORE THEY COVER IT.

The fact that students learn in different, personally adaptive ways is now beyond dispute. In all phases of teaching, but especially in the readiness phase, teachers face the formidable challenge of what to do about learning differences in classrooms. With all these variations in learners, how can a teacher create lessons that meet the needs of such a wide range of learning preferences? Roland Barth, a noted educational author, gives a clue. He suggests that teachers use learner differences to create a shared array of classroom assets. In such classrooms learners capitalize on their fundamental differences by agreeing to learn with and from each other. In this way learning differences, rather than being treated as liabilities, become strengths.

Mutual respect is therefore an essential condition of the readiness phase of learning. In a classroom where mutual respect is cultivated, learners test their ideas in dialogue with others. Learning is made public through collaborative knowledge building. Instruction is explicitly designed to draw forth student opinions and ideas as a basis for connecting prior knowledge and experience to new learning. More learners succeed in classrooms that honor learning differences and foster mutual respect. Momentum for learning is a natural by-product in classrooms that prepare learners for success.

Several decades ago, now-noted educational visionary Jerome Bruner wrote an essay about momentum and learning that contains important clues about the readiness phase of learning. In this essay, "The Will to Learn," Bruner (1996) asserted, "Learning is so deeply ingrained in man that it is virtually involuntary." For Bruner, humans learn automatically when curiosity combines with the instinctive drive to attain competence. Whenever learners experience dissonance in the form of a problem whose solution is unclear and they are given a reasonable process for achieving that solution, the learning

The whole art of teaching is only the art of awakening the natural curiosity of young minds for the purpose of satisfying it afterwards.

— Anatole France

MINDSHIFT: *Curiosity is nature's way of reminding us that learning is good for us.*

process is meaningfully initiated. Schools that activate interest, that connect to prior knowledge, that communicate expectations and frame the content as integral parts of classroom organization, and that treat learners as though they know more than they think they know, create momentum for sustaining and enjoying future learning.

GETTING STARTED

GETTING STARTED

How do teachers in our school use readiness activities to prepare students for successful participation in new learning?

GETTING STARTED

How do teachers in our school communicate, in advance, expectations for successful participation in learning activities?

How do teachers in our school encourage learners to publicly risk the challenges of new learning?

The mediocre teacher tells.
The good teacher explains.
The superior teacher demonstrates.
The great teacher inspires.

—William Arthur Ward

LOOKING DEEPER

WHAT DO YOU SEE IN CLASSROOMS WHERE READINESS, PREPARING LEARNERS FOR SUCCESS, IS A NONNEGOTIABLE COMPONENT OF CLASSROOM TEACHING?

Place a check indicating an aspect of your school program that is particularly effective.

LEARNER READINESS IN CLASSROOMS: PRODUCTS, ACTIVITIES, AND ARTIFACTS

__ Active-listening activities

__ Advance organizers

__ Anticipatory set activities

__ Chapter tours

__ Content pacing guides

__ Cooperative learning activities

__ Dramatizations

__ Exploratory discussions

__ Guest speakers

__ Interactive Internet whiteboards

__ Interdisciplinary exploration activities

__ KWL charts

__ Mind maps

__ Multisensory activities

__ Opinion polls and surveys

__ Personal journal writing

__ Posters depicting what students will learn

__ PowerPoint presentations

__ Preassessment activities

__ Relational diagrams

__ Role-play

__ Show and tell

__ Storytelling/comedy

__ Student art projects/poetry

__ Tablet PCs

__ Video presentations

__ Word walls

__ Other (describe)

Notes:

Discuss evidence of your assessment.

THE PEDAGOGY OF LEARNER READINESS *(what the teacher does)*

__ *Establish a reason/rationale for learning*

__ *Connect to existing levels of student understanding*

__ *Guide student curiosity and use exploratory discussion to build mutual respect*

__ *Clarify misconceptions*

__ *Explain expectations and schedules for new learning*

__ *Provide a "road map" for new learning using visual advance organizers*

__ *Other (describe)*

Notes:

Discuss evidence of your assessment.

THE VERBS OF LEARNER READINESS *(what the students are doing)*

__ *Brainstorming*

__ *Describing*

__ *Generating questions*

__ *Inferring*

__ *Listening*

__ *Observing*

__ *Perspective taking*

__ *Previewing content*

__ *Questioning*

__ *Reflecting*

__ *Relating*

__ *Restating*

__ *Sharing opinions*

__ *Surveying*

__ *Other (describe)*

Notes:

Discuss evidence of your assessment.

WHAT ARE THE EXISTING STRENGTHS OF YOUR SCHOOL WITH REGARD TO THE READINESS PHASE OF TEACHING?

__ *Learning activities that invite student curiosity and interest*

__ *Teacher enthusiasm for subject matter*

__ *Verbal exchanges and questions that minimize student misconceptions*

__ *Discussions that link existing knowledge and new learning*

__ *Published criteria for assessing student success*

__ *Printed expectations for specific learning tasks*

__ *Distribution of content pacing guides*

__ *Use of visual advance organizers to frame the content*

__ *Grouping practices that require students to share their thoughts and help each other*

WHAT CAN BE DONE TO CONVINCE TEACHERS NOT TO SKIP OR RUSH THROUGH THE READINESS PHASE OF TEACHING?

TAKING ACTION

TASK ONE: WALK-THRU

Directions: Complete several readiness Walk-Thru templates to get a sense of how teachers in your school prepare students for purposeful learning.

See Figure 7.1

Note Well: Remember a Walk-Thru is not a formal observation. It has nothing to do with the evaluation of teaching. The goal of the Walk-Thru is to increase shared meanings among faculty members about how promising strategies for setting the stage for meaningful learning might be shared and refined by teachers.

Walk-Thrus are designed to be completed in a very short period of time, even in passing.

First Note: What Works Now:
_____
_____
_____
_____

Then list specific barriers to incorporating Readiness Activities in classroom:
_____
_____
_____
_____

TASK TWO: READINESS RUBRIC

Directions: Complete the Readiness Rubric on the following pages and informally discuss your assessment with colleagues.

Based upon recent observations, the following is appropriate:

• Celebrate and recognize exemplary readiness strategy use throughout the school

• Organize faculty study group teams to support experimentation with readiness strategies in classrooms

• Ask for assistance on readiness use from district-level support professionals

• Other

See Figure 7.2

CLASSROOM WALK-THRU

READINESS: PREPARING LEARNERS FOR SUCCESS

CONTENT TAUGHT _____

_____

DATE _____

INSIGHTS NOTED:

- ESTABLISH A RATIONALE
- ACTIVATE INTEREST
- CONNECT TO PRIOR LEARNING
- COMMUNICATE EXPECTATIONS
- FRAME THE CONTENT

ACTIVITIES/RESOURCES

ACTIVITIES/RESOURCES OBSERVED:

- LEARNING LOGS/PLANNERS
- ADVANCE ORGANIZERS
- UNIT GUIDES/POSTED EXPECTATIONS
- PREVIEW ACTIVITIES
- VISUAL AIDS
- DISCUSSION GROUPS
- OTHER: _____

NOTE WELL: This Walk-Thru is intended to promote shared meaning about best practice in teaching; it should never be used to evaluate teacher performance.

Figure 7.1

READINESS RUBRIC

SETTING THE STAGE FOR: MEANINGFUL LEARNING

Check the appropriate level of implementation

Establish a rationale for learning by using personal experience and prior knowledge as an important connection to new learning, and framing that learning in expected outcomes.

GUIDING PRINCIPLE:

New learning is best introduced and initiated in a context that is framed by personal experience and explained in light of expected outcomes.

1
Teachers in our school rarely use the readiness techniques described in this chapter.

2
Teachers in our school sometimes use the readiness techniques described in this chapter.

3
Teachers in our school often use the readiness techniques described in this chapter.

4
Teachers in our school always use the readiness techniques described in this chapter.

Reliable Indicators:

- Modeled enthusiasm for learning
- Arousal of student interest & attention
- Classroom discussions of connections to previous lessons & prior knowledge
- Use of advance organizations, study questions, & predictions to prepare students for new learning

Figure 7.2

TASK THREE: SHARE FAIR MONTH – WEEK ONE

Group teachers into voluntary pairs or triads and ask them to discuss the Readiness Phase as described in Mindful Teaching, share success stories, and offer each other suggestions about how to better prepare students for meaningful learning.

FIRST: **Select one month toward the end of the school year for sharing classroom artifacts and resources.**

May is preferred because high-stakes tests are usually completed by then, and May is a time in the school year when plans for the next school year become actionable.

NOW: **In Week One, select one (or several) of the following Mindful Teaching strategies in the Readiness Phase of teaching as described here and share classroom examples, successful activities, and resources that can be used to increase the quality of teaching in the school.**

Recruit parent volunteers to help organize materials for display and facilitate their availability to interested teachers.

Designate the first week of Share Fair month for teachers to exchange ideas and resources about improving the Readiness Phase of classroom teaching.

Create a safe space in the school where classroom artifacts, resources, and activities can be displayed and reviewed by faculty members.

FINALLY: **Hold periodic meetings for teachers to explain and share these ideas and resources.** These meetings can be organized as follows:

- By departments
- By teaching teams
- By non-teaching periods
- By grade levels
- By subject area
- By interest
- By faculty

Subsequent weeks will address the delivery, performance, and transfer phases of Mindful Teaching.

Note: In the first week of Share Fair it is very important to connect resources and activities to the Readiness Phase of Mindful Teaching as follows:

- *Activating interest*
- *Connecting to prior knowledge*
- *Communicating expectations*
- *Framing the content*

MAKING SENSE

THE VOCABULARY OF LEARNER READINESS

ADVANCE ORGANIZERS

are visual representations or brief textual passages that orient learners to subject matter and relate to the preexisting knowledge learners already have. Advance Organizers provide learners with a "big picture" of the content. They help learners build, organize, and recognize key concepts in the material to be learned. They also help learners form conceptual associations that facilitate future learning.

ANTICIPATORY SET

is an introductory teaching strategy that is used to connect the experiences of the students to the goals of the lesson. Sometimes called a "hook" to grab the student's attention, anticipatory set activities help students to focus their awareness on the rationale for the lesson and create an organizing framework for the ideas, principles, or information that is to follow.

CHAPTER TOURS

are guided surveys of the material that call attention to the main ideas of the chapter, point out important themes, and help learners recognize how the author highlights the most important material.

Only when we are stopped in our tracks by a problem or situation that forces us to think or rethink is there the possibility of new learning.

—Eric Jensen

COGNITIVE DISSONANCE

is a state of uneasiness that results from trying to resolve contradictory or otherwise incompatible ideas, attitudes, or beliefs. The experience of dissonance naturally initiates the learning process.

EXPLORATORY DISCUSSIONS

are classroom discussions that are used primarily to orient learners to new subject matter to be learned. Exploratory discussions enable the teacher to correct misconceptions, to focus on critical attributes, and to introduce new concepts. Exploratory discussions emphasize appropriate rather than correct responses.

INTERDISCIPLINARY DISCUSSIONS

are classroom discussions that invite students to explore the connection between what is being learned in one subject and what has previously been learned in other disciplines. Interdisciplinary Discussions expand and enhance student memory and retrieval by forming relevant webs of connected information.

K-W-L CHARTS (KNOW-WANT TO KNOW-LEARNED)

are graphic organizers that juxtapose what a learner knows, wants to know, and has learned. The chart functions as a comparative study reference and can be used by the teacher to highlight the relevance of subject matter.

MIND MAPS

are visual patterns of information that provide a framework for depicting the relatedness of ideas or information. They work on both verbal and nonverbal levels. Mind Maps quickly, vividly, and accurately help learners engage both hemispheres of the brain to form a thinking map of concepts embedded in subject matter.

RELATIONAL DIAGRAMS

are closed figures that show the pattern of overlap between classes of objects, events, or abstractions. Relational diagrams help learners discriminate between and label related terms. Relational diagrams are useful in instigating and focusing classroom discussions. They help clarify what students are thinking.

THUMBNAIL SKETCH

Directions: Review the ideas and strategies discussed in this chapter. Create a saying, draw a symbol, or write a quote that can be used to draw attention to your school's commitment to improve the Readiness Phase of classroom teaching. Be creative and have fun.

LOOKING WIDER

SUGGESTED READINGS

Barth, Roland S., "Improving Schools From Within," Jossey-Bass Publishers, 1990

Barth, Roland S., "Learning by Heart," John Wiley & Sons, Inc., 2001

Bruner, Jerome S., "The Process of Education," Harvard University Press, 1977

Bruner, Jerome S., "The Will to Learn," Actual Minds, Possible Worlds (The Jerusalem Harvard Lectures)

Buehl, Doug, "Classroom Strategies for Interactive Learning," International Reading Association, Inc., 2001

Friedman, Myles I., "Ensuring Student Success: A Handbook of Evidence-Based Strategies," The Institute for Evidence-Based Decision-Making in Education, Inc., 2000

Harmin, Merrill, "Inspiring Active Learning," Association for Supervision and Curriculum Development, 1994

Zull, James E., "The Art of Changing the Brain," Stylus Publishing, LLC, 2002

SIGNS OF SUCCESS WORTH FIGHTING FOR

- *Published content pacing guides*
- *Frequent preassessment of student understanding*
- *Use of advance organizers and graphic organizers to frame difficult content*
- *Availability of high-interest materials*
- *Classroom discussion that focuses on linking prior knowledge to new learning*

Where interest appears,
achievement follows.

—Alfie Kohn

DISCUSSION WEB
Share your ideas

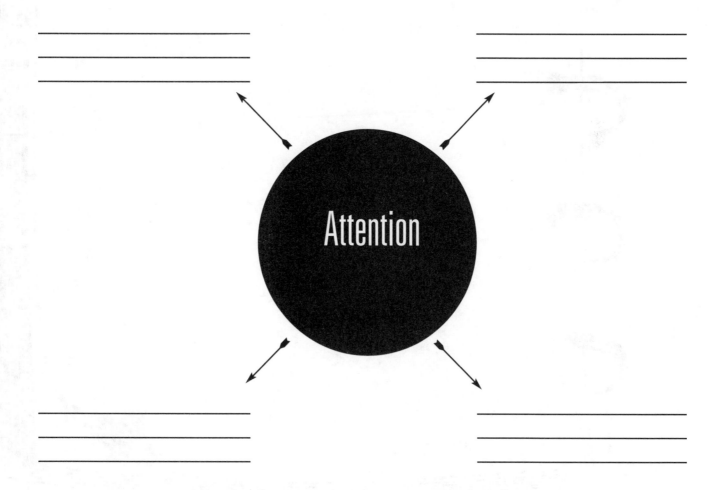

CREATING A LEARNING PLACE

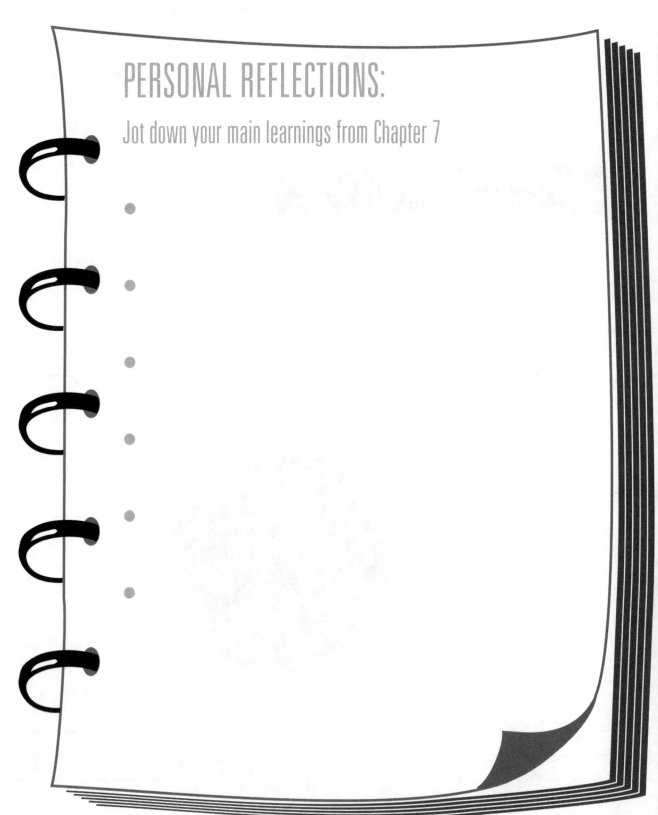

PERSONAL REFLECTIONS:

Jot down your main learnings from Chapter 7

CHAPTER EIGHT: ENGAGING STUDENT THINKING

ESSENTIAL QUESTION:

What can classroom teachers do to enliven the exchange of ideas and draw student attention to relevant, meaningful content?

BIG IDEA —WHEN SUBJECT MATTER IS USED TO ENLIVEN THINKING AND CREATE A LARGER CONTEXT FOR KNOWING, EXPERIENCING, AND UNDERSTANDING THE WORLD, MORE STUDENTS GET "TURNED ON" TO SCHOOL.

The Delivery Phase of teaching places considerable demand on a student's ability to acquire, organize, and consolidate new ideas to meaning. Without the careful guidance of a vigilant teacher, many less-able students quietly retreat into themselves during this phase of learning. However, in classrooms where teachers use thought-provoking questions, solicit student opinions about content, probe student understanding, and define, explain, relate, and recap information to be learned, participatory learning is virtually guaranteed for most, if not all, students.

The person doing the thinking is the person doing the learning.

—Anonymous

An artfully delivered interactive lecture is a thing of beauty. And while there is no one best way to lecture, research supports the use of several teaching practices that activate and engage student thinking and establish a positive, stimulating, and encouraging classroom learning climate during the all-lecture phase of teaching. Some of these teaching practices are the use of interactive dialogue and note-taking techniques, cuing and redirection, probing with questions, affirming understanding, and lengthening wait time.

Lectures that enliven learning begin with a brief sampling of what is engaging, relevant, and meaningful in the content. The intention here is to lead students to construct a framework of related ideas that will eventually lead to greater levels of understanding. Most of all, the interactive lecture provides a context for teachers to share their enthusiasm for the value and relevance of learning the subject matter.

Key components of an interactive lecture include the following:
- **Opening**—an invitation to learn something meaningful
- **Cuing**—a heads up when something is particularly important
- **Lecturing**—organized explanation of key ideas with notes
- **Probing with questions**—redirecting and clarifying student thinking
- **Exchanging meanings**—defining, explaining, relating, and recapping information
- **Affirming understanding**—consolidating understanding and preparing for future learning challenges

OPENING

As teachers prepare to lecture on new subject matter, the lesson should be organized to engage students in active listening, personal translation, and responding activities that help them "make sense" of how ideas in this content are organized for meaning. Several strategies for engaging student thinking during the introductory phase of an interactive lecture include the following:
- Posing thought-provoking questions about the topic
- Soliciting student responses to statements about the content
- Asking students to complete incomplete statements about the subject matter
- Opening the lecture with an outlandish statement that is deliberately false and having students react
- Beginning the lecture with "Did you know?" or "Consider this" statements

CUING

Cuing and questioning are the heart of interactive lectures. Interactive lectures seek to deepen understanding and engage student thinking. Properly placed test events and rhetorical questions posed to the entire class in an effort to focus student thinking allow teachers to keep the lecture briskly paced without interruption. Examples of test events include the following: What do you think life would be like without…? or How could you have predicted this outcome…? Verbal cues such as, Please pay particular attention to… You will need to know… Look closely at… Direct your attention to…. Call student attention to a specific aspect of content and also help both the teacher and the learner stay on track. Robert Marzano (2001) in his recent book, *Classroom Instruction that Works*, cites research in classrooms that suggests that cuing and questioning might account for as much as 80% of what occurs in classrooms on a given day. It's no wonder that these teaching competencies are considered vital components of Mindful Teaching.

LECTURING AND INTERACTIVE NOTE TAKING

The actual delivery of instruction was once a teacher-dominated oratory given to help students note and remember important content. But it has evolved into a guided, interactive exchange of ideas that has as its end the construction of important meanings related to a specific topic. Thus the traditional scene of a teacher standing at the lectern giving notes with students quietly taking down every word has given way to an interactive dialogue that incorporates new information, questions, clarifications, and explanations of meanings. The great advantage of the interactive lecture is the active engagement of learners with content.

Walter Pauk, noted professor at Cornell University and author of the widely acclaimed *How to Study in College*, has written extensively on the complementary nature of lecturing and interactive note taking. **His Cornell Method provides a format for combining active listening, note taking, and visual thinking that helps students accumulate information in an orderly systematic way, and provides teachers with a template for engaging student thinking during the lecture.** Unlike traditional notes that seek to capture exactly what the teacher says, Cornell Notes are evolving translations of lecture content and textbook material that provide learners with a written record of what they are learning.

Using the Cornell Method, students divide a notes page into three distinct areas for gathering information about subject matter. These areas are the cue column, the notes column and the summary area. By drawing a line two inches from the left margin students divide their notes page into a two-inch cue column on the left and a six-inch notes column on the right. The summary area is then added by drawing a horizontal line two inches from the bottom of the page.

CORNELL NOTES

CUE COLUMN

SUMMARY BOX

Personalized translations of the salient ideas of a lecture or notes from a reading of a textbook chapter are then placed in the notes column. As students are taking notes, the cue column remains empty. However, notes are not complete until the cue column is filled in. During a review of the notes students are encouraged to place key words, questions, and "big picture" association statements that provide an "at-a-glance" record of what is recorded in the notes column. By leaving space between entries in the notes column, students can also continually upgrade their notes. Finally, summary questions are added in the summary area once the cue column is completed.

Using the Cornell Notes template as a guide, teachers can add structure to their lectures by making overheads with key ideas written in the cue column. As students learn this method, they become increasingly less dependent upon the teacher for identifying the key concepts.

Aided by recent advances in technology, interactive note-taking tools have evolved beyond paper and pencil formats. For a computer-generated program of interactive note taking tools and learning prompts including Cornell formats, graphic organizers, self-testing guides, and rapid search reference sources, see StudyWhiz.com.

PROBING WITH QUESTIONS

A basic premise of Mindful Teaching is that learning flourishes in classrooms where students have opportunities to wrestle with uncertainties, exchange ideas, and benefit from the perspectives of others. To this end, teachers are encouraged to follow the introduction of new ideas with a brief, focused question-feedback exchange. During this exchange, teachers should seize the opportunity to correct lingering misconceptions, draw student attention to important ideas, provide timely feedback, and probe student understanding.

For decades teachers have used the work of Benjamin Bloom and his Taxonomy of Educational Objectives to frame questions and learning tasks for use in classrooms. The six levels of learning identified in Bloom's Taxonomy—knowledge, comprehension, application, analysis, synthesis, and evaluation—are intended to describe six increasingly complex levels of thinking. Thus, according to Bloom, there are increasingly complex levels of thinking that students must master as they develop cognitively. Generally, teachers are encouraged to begin probing student understanding by starting with knowledge-level questions and moving progressively upward through the taxonomy to evaluation. A brief description of Benjamin Bloom's Taxonomy and its application to education is as follows:

Evaluation – the ability to make a judgment based upon criteria

- Compare and contrast ideas
- Attribute value
- Make decisions based on reasoned argument
- Verify reliability of evidence
- Affirm subjective validity claims

What would constitute a reasonable justification for a nation to go to war?

Synthesis – the ability to combine ideas in meaningful ways

- Create new meanings by combining existing ideas
- Generalize from given facts
- Relate knowledge from several areas
- Predict, draw conclusions

What historical events could have been used to predict the Japanese decision to bomb Pearl Harbor?

Analysis – the ability to separate knowledge into component parts

- Identifying structure
- Specifying parts
- Recognition of patterns and relationships
- Understanding organization

Distinguish between the new, waxing crescent, first quarter, waxing gibbous, full, waning gibbous, last quarter, and waning crescent phases of the moon.

Application – the ability to use new ideas in new situations

- Use information
- Use methods, concepts, theories in new situations
- Solve problems using required skills or knowledge
- Demonstrate skills development

How would you write the expression "Every cloud has a silver lining" in if-then form?

Comprehension – the ability to grasp meaning

- Understanding information
- Restate ideas in ways that make sense
- Translate knowledge
- Interpret facts, compare, contrast
- Order, group, infer causes
- Predict consequences

Explain how a bill becomes law.

Knowledge – the ability to recognize and recall information

- Observation and recall of information
- Knowledge of dates, events, places
- Knowledge of major ideas

List and define the major organs of the human body.

EXCHANGING MEANINGS

Some of the most rewarding moments of teaching happen when students express and explain their ideas about what content means to them. Exchanging ideas and building collaborative knowledge are integral components of interactive lectures. **Helping students become comfortable and skillful in explaining and organizing their thoughts is yet another goal of Mindful Teaching.**

In the Delivery Phase of teaching, student thinking is enhanced when teachers use an organizing principle to ensure that their lectures are clear and focused. One such organizing principle is to determine, in advance of a lecture, What do I want students to be able to do with the content I am teaching? Do I want students to define and give examples of the ideas and information I am teaching? Do I want students to explain the origins of these ideas and what they mean? Do I want students to relate ideas to other ideas? Do I want students to summarize their understanding of content? These four questions can be used to encourage students to exchange ideas and model different ways of thinking.

In 1974, Mary Budd Rowe conducted extensive research on the quality of discourse in science classes. Since then her studies have been replicated with extraordinarily consistent results. Her research confirmed that many classroom teachers unknowingly failed to provide sufficient time for students to frame responses to questions in class. By drawing attention to this problem and suggesting that teachers provide at least three seconds "wait time" for students to respond to questions, five important things happen:

- The level of student discourse increases significantly
- Student responses are more likely to be given in whole statements
- Speculative thinking increases
- Student questions increase
- Student performance improves.

AFFIRMING

Affirming is the final stage of the interactive lecture. In the affirming stage teachers summarize what has been taught and collect evidence that students are either ready to move to the application phase of learning or need additional review and reteaching.

The affirming stage of the interactive lecture also provides a context for students to engage in self-assessing their present understanding. Activities like making a statement regarding the topic and asking learners by a show of hands to agree or disagree can help affirm understanding and provide opportunities for teachers to provide timely feedback. Taking this activity one step farther, teachers could make a statement about content and ask students to go to one of the four corners of the room depending upon their degree of agreement or disagreement with a statement. One corner of the room is designated for those who slightly agree, another for those who strongly agree, and the two others being levels in between.

GETTING STARTED

GETTING STARTED

How do teachers in our school use verbal and visual cues to engage student thinking during lectures?

GETTING STARTED

How do teachers in our school probe student learning and provide timely feedback during content lectures?

How do teachers in our school review and reteach content?

How do teachers in our school encourage students to self-assess their current level of understanding and affirm their progress?

LOOKING DEEPER

WHAT DO YOU SEE IN SCHOOLS WHERE ENGAGING STUDENT THINKING IS A NONNEGOTIABLE COMPONENT OF THE DELIVERY PHASE OF TEACHING?

Place a check indicating an aspect of your school program that is particularly effective.

ENGAGING STUDENT THINKING IN CLASSROOMS: PRODUCTS, ACTIVITIES, AND ARTIFACTS

___ Book reviews

___ Classification tasks

___ Classroom notes

___ Compare and contrast visuals

___ Computers in classrooms

___ Content charts

___ Course outlines

___ Curriculum target lists

___ Deductive strategies

___ Demonstrations

___ Direct instruction

___ Flow charts

___ Formal research

___ Formal writing

___ Guest lecturer

___ Guest speakers

___ Individual self-test activities

___ Informative bulletin boards

___ Informative video

___ Interactive CDs

___ Internet projectors

___ Pretest materials

___ PowerPoint presentations

___ Schema diagrams

___ Serial order tasks

___ Socratic questions

___ Tablet PCs

___ Test events

___ Text summaries

___ Theoretical discussions

___ Timelines

___ Venn diagrams

___ Weekly assignment planners

Notes:

Discuss evidence of your assessment.

THE PEDAGOGY OF ENGAGING STUDENT THINKING
(what the teacher is doing)

___ *Identify key concepts*

___ *Systematically direct student attention to similarities and differences*

___ *Define, explain, exchange, model, and relate important ideas*

___ *Probe with questions and provide feedback*

___ *Impose formal structure on material to be learned*

___ *Guide student categorization/organization of ideas for future use*

Notes:

Discuss evidence of your assessment.

THE VERBS OF ENGAGING STUDENT THINKING
(what the kids are doing)

___ *Analyzing*

___ *Comparing*

___ *Consolidating*

___ *Contrasting*

___ *Deriving*

___ *Discriminating*

___ *Hypothesizing*

___ *Identifying parts*

___ *Making notes*

___ *Naming (differences)*

___ *Ordering*

___ *Organizing*

___ *Prioritizing*

___ *Reading*

___ *Reasoning*

___ *Specifying*

___ *Structuring*

___ *Translating*

___ *Visually connecting content (similarities)*

Notes:

Discuss evidence of your assessment.

TAKING ACTION

TASK ONE: WALK-THRU

Directions: Complete several Delivery Phase Walk-Thru templates to get a sense of how teachers in your school engage student thinking during the instructional Delivery Phase of teaching.

See Figure 8.1

First Note: What Works Now:

_____

_____

_____

_____

Then list specific barriers to incorporating Delivery Activities in classroom:

_____

_____

_____

_____

TASK TWO: DELIVERY RUBRIC

Directions: Complete the Delivery Rubric below and informally discuss your assessment with colleagues. Based upon recent observations, the following is appropriate:

- Celebrate and recognize exemplary delivery strategy use throughout the school

- Organize faculty study-group teams to support experimentation with delivery strategies in classrooms

- Ask for assistance on delivery use from district-level support professionals

- Other

See Figure 8.2

CLASSROOM WALK-THRU

DELIVERY: ENGAGING LEARNER THINKING

CONTENT TAUGHT _____
_____
DATE _____

IDENTIFYING KEY CONCEPTS

- DEFINE
- EXPLAIN
- RELATE
- EXCHANGE
- PROBE WITH QUESTIONS
- SUMMARIZE

INSIGHTS NOTED:

ACTIVITIES/RESOURCES

- NOTE TAKING
- GUIDE BOOKS
- DIRECT INSTRUCTION
- LECTURE
- DEMONSTRATIONS
- VIDEO/TECHNOLOGY
- GUEST SPEAKER
- OTHER: _____

ACTIVITIES/RESOURCES OBSERVED:

NOTE WELL: This Walk-Thru is intended to promote shared meaning about best practice in teaching; it should never be used to evaluate teacher performance.

Figure 8.1

DELIVERY RUBRIC

DEEPENING LEARNER UNDERSTANDING

Exchanging ideas and making critical sense of new learning.

Check the appropriate level of implementation.

GUIDING PRINCIPLE:
All formal learning involves understanding ideas embedded in a knowledge system. In classrooms where this knowledge is clearly defined, organized, and linked to previous knowledge, learning is enhanced.

1
Teachers in our school rarely use the interactive lecture strategies techniques described in this chapter.

2
Teachers in our school sometimes use the interactive lecture techniques described in this chapter.

3
Teachers in our school often use the interactive lecture techniques described in this chapter.

4
Teachers in our school always use the interactive lecture techniques described in this chapter.

Reliable Indicators:

- General overview and rationale for lesson content
- Whole-group instruction, with brisk consistent exchange of key ideas
- Focused questions with clarification and feedback
- Verbal praise for active participation
- "Wait time" for student response
- Humor
- Closing summary

Figure 8.2

TASK THREE: SHARE FAIR MONTH – WEEK TWO

Group teachers into voluntary pairs or triads and ask them to discuss the Delivery Phase as described in Mindful Teaching and share success stories, and offer each other suggestions about how to better prepare students for meaningful learning.

FIRST: **Designate Week Two of Share Fair month to the Delivery Phase of Mindful Teaching.**

NOW: **Ask teachers to collect Delivery Phase-related classroom examples, activities, and resources that can be shared with other faculty members to increase the quality of teaching in the school.**

FINALLY: **Hold periodic meetings for teachers to explain and share these ideas and resources.** These meetings can be organized as follows:

- By departments
- By teaching teams
- By nonteaching periods
- By grade levels
- By subject area
- By interest
- By faculty

Note: In the second week of Share Fair it is very important to connect resources and activities to the following:

- *Exchanging ideas*
- *Probing with questions*
- *Affirming understanding*

Remember each phase of Mindful Teaching will have its own week.

MAKING SENSE

THE VOCABULARY OF CONTENT DELIVERY

BLOOM'S TAXONOMY

is a taxonomy for identifying the cognitive complexity of questions that commonly occur in educational settings. The taxonomy provides a useful structure for organizing and framing interactive dialogue in classrooms.

CORNELL NOTES

are a specialized system for capturing the important elements of classroom lectures in ways that model a natural cycle of learning. Developed by Walter Pauk at Cornell University, this system, described in his book *How to Study in College*, has been adopted by countless colleges and universities and is also used by many forward-thinking secondary teachers.

DEFINING QUESTIONS

focus on characterizing ideas, identifying critical attributes, giving examples, and listing specific functions.

EXPLAINING QUESTIONS

elicit a more complete understanding of ideas that incorporates the origins and rationale for important ideas.

RECAPPING

is a teaching strategy that draws student attention to what they know and what they need to learn.

RELATING QUESTIONS

focus on the similarities in ideas by grouping them by similar criteria, i.e., functions, attributes, characteristics, even levels of difficulties.

RHETORICAL QUESTIONS

are statements that are formulated as questions but that are not supposed to be answered. The rhetorical question is usually defined as any question asked for a purpose other than to obtain the information the question asks.

TEST EVENT

is an interactive lecture strategy that is used to refocus student attention and keep all students actively engaged in thinking about the topic. During the lecture, the teacher periodically asks the entire class to respond to a statement by raising their hand as a sign they agree with the statement. For example, during a lecture on weather, a teacher might say, "Raise your hand if you agree that hurricanes are the most dangerous natural disaster." Following the statement the teacher would then ask a specific student to explain why they agree or disagree.

VENN DIAGRAMS

are graphic representations of two or more overlapping circles. They are often used in mathematics to show relationships between sets. In Language Arts instruction, Venn diagrams are useful for examining similarities and differences in characters, stories, poems, etc.

They are frequently used as a prewriting activity to enable students to organize thoughts or textual quotations prior to writing a compare/contrast essay. This activity enables students to visually organize similarities and differences.

VERBAL AND VISUAL CUES

are directions and signals for students to give special emphasis to salient ideas. These cues are given by the teacher to call learners to a specific action; for example, "please note," or "place a star next to the definition of." These cues keep momentum going during interactive lectures and help both the teacher and learner direct attention and jump-start thinking.

WAIT TIME

is the amount of time that elapses between an instructor-initiated question and the next verbal behavior (e.g., a student response or question, the instructor talks again). If the wait time is very brief, this encourages students, especially those who are unsure of their answers, to respond with one-word answers or refuse to answer.

LOOKING WIDER

SUGGESTED READINGS

Bloom, Benjamin S., "Taxonomy of Educational Objectives, Handbook 1: Cognitive Domain," Addison-Wesley Publishing Company, 1956

Brandt, Ron, "Powerful Learning," Association for Supervision and Curriculum Development, 1998

Friedman, Myles I., and Fisher, Steven P., "Handbook on Effective Instructional Strategies: Evidence for Decision-Making," The Institute for Evidence-Based Decision-Making in Education, Inc., 1998

Marzano, Robert J., "Classroom Instruction That Works," Association for Supervision and Curriculum Development, 2001

National Research Council, Bransford, John D., et al., "How People Learn," National Academy Press, 2000

Pauk, Walter, "How to Study in College," Houghton Mifflin Company, 2004

Perkins, David, "Smart Schools," The Free Press, 1992

Rowe, Mary Budd, "Teaching Science as Continuous Inquiry: A Basic," 2nd Edition, McGraw-Hill, 1978

White, Richard, and Gunstone, Richard, "Probing Understanding," The Falmer Press, 1998

SIGNS OF SUCCESS WORTH FIGHTING FOR

- *Interactive lectures and personalized note taking*
- *Probing with questions and feedback*
- *Frequent paraphrasing of student understanding*
- *Reteaching*
- *Reading across content areas*

Beyond learning about a subject, students will need lessons that enable them to experience directly the inquiries, arguments, applications, and points of view underneath the facts and opinions they learn if they are to understand them.

— Grant Wiggins
and Jay McTighe

CREATING A LEARNING PLACE

PERSONAL REFLECTIONS:

Jot down your main learnings from Chapter 8

CHAPTER NINE: SUPPORTING STUDENT PERFORMANCE

ESSENTIAL QUESTION:

What can classroom teachers do to guide students to use information learned in the Delivery Phase of instruction to solve relevant problems, grapple with challenging questions, and demonstrate deeper levels of understanding?

BIG IDEA — IN MINDFUL CLASSROOMS, THE SYMBIOTIC RELATIONSHIP BETWEEN ACQUIRING KNOWLEDGE AND USING KNOWLEDGE TO DEEPEN UNDERSTANDING IS AFFIRMED DAILY.

Learners of all ages are more motivated when they can see the usefulness of what they are learning and when they can use that information to do something that has impact on others—especially their local community.

—John D. Bransford

MINDSHIFT: *The link between knowing and understanding is "hand-made."*

We now know that learners soon forget knowledge that they do not put to use. Students taught solely by lecture gain understanding slowly and at a lower level when compared to those taught to extend acquired knowledge through active experimentation. In the Performance Phase of Mindful Teaching, teachers and students put the knowledge gained in the Delivery Phase of Mindful Teaching to work.

The Performance Phase of Mindful Teaching is about creating knowledge and understanding from within. Performance here is, therefore, synonymous with solving relevant problems, illustrating ideas, grappling with challenging questions, defending opinions, exploring alternative points of view, using technology interactively, conducting experiments, writing in various forms, self-testing, improving, and monitoring performance. Group work, self-directed learning, and performance assessment activities take center stage during the Performance Phase of Mindful Teaching.

Grant Wiggins and Jay McTighe have written about learning tasks that foster understanding. They offer six facets of understanding that are particularly useful as organizing principles for the Performance Phase of Mindful Teaching:

FACETS OF UNDERSTANDING

Explanation: generating examples that help explain the key ideas in the content, grappling with essential questions, sharing understanding, and explaining how problems might be solved.
Basic criteria = accuracy

Application: using content in ways that give evidence of knowledge, testing ideas for validity, building models and representations of ideas, conducting experiments, self-adjusting, and/or demonstrating skill.
Basic criteria = effectiveness

Interpretation: creating a coherent, interesting account (or story) of the content, making sense of the facts, pointing out examples from other sources, and illuminating a personal interpretation of their present level of understanding.
Basic criteria = meaningful representation

Perspective Taking: exposing questionable or unexamined assumptions, placing ideas in context, challenging conclusions and implications, examining alternative theories, and considering diverse points of view.
Basic criteria = revealing points of view

Empathy: appreciating differences, learning to grasp the world from someone else's point of view, using imagination to see and feel as others do, embracing insights that are subjective or aesthetic by finding what is plausible, sensible, or meaningful in the ideas and actions of others, seeking to understand what is different, and showing respect for people different from ourselves.
Basic criteria = perceptive insights

Self-Knowledge: questioning personal understanding, knowing personal limits, examining prejudices, recognizing metacognitive strengths and achievements, and accepting feedback and criticism without defensiveness.
Basic criteria = self-adjusted planning

The function of a genius is not to give new answers, but to pose new questions which time and mediocrity can resolve.

——Hugh Trevor-Roper

In today's classrooms, teachers who are successful guide students through several phases of learning that balance the acquisition of organized sets of facts and skills with a meaningful exploration of why, when, and how those facts and skills can be used to create deeper levels of understanding. Supporting student performance through high-involvement guided practice kicks learning and the brain into high gear.

Think about a grand orchestra preparing to play a symphony. The parallels to Mindful Teaching are striking. For example, before one note is sounded the orchestra leader must guarantee that all players know exactly what will be expected of them as the orchestra prepares for opening night. He or she must also guarantee that each player is properly prepared to understand his or her directions and work successfully with others to guarantee success. Finally, he or she must draw out and correct misconceptions players have as to their role in playing the piece. The orchestra is now READY to take instruction.

For a symphony orchestra, the DELIVERY of instruction takes the form of calling out specific differences in the composition of the music, modeling how these differences make this work unique, teaching relevant techniques, providing suggestions and feedback for interpreting the music notations, and guiding collective understanding of how the music fits together. Without these common understandings the orchestra could not even attempt its rendition of the work.

I hear and I forget.
I see and I remember.
I do and I understand.

—Chinese proverb

Up to this point the role of the orchestra leader (teacher) has been the preparation of players and the transfer of knowledge and information orchestra members will need to play the symphony. Players for their part have been taking in information and clarifying the salient techniques and understandings embedded in this particular symphony.

Now, everything changes. Players are ready to refine their understandings and techniques and translate them into PERFORMANCES. Clarinetists refine their technique and phrasing, percussionists experiment with timing, and trumpets work on tone. The orchestra leader now becomes a guide on the side assisting each group with its rehearsal sets providing feedback and support where necessary. Control of the learning task passes from the orchestra leader to the group and then to the individual. New options for playing the symphony appear as everyone works to prepare for the dress rehearsal. This is the Performance Phase of this symphony's learning cycle. The players have changed from receivers to producers.

The goal of the Performance Phase of any teaching cycle is simulating and re-simulating the dress rehearsal. In the dress rehearsal everything becomes public. Things come together in ways that invite experimentation, problem solving, solution finding, and self-appraisal. Without the Performance Phase, knowledge and information remain separate from the learner. Performances take learning deeper and wider.

GROUPING FOR PERFORMANCES

Any discussion about the Performance Phase of Mindful Teaching must include suggestions for flexible student grouping practices. These grouping practices are called "flexible" because they are organized around student interest, student need, or mixed abilities. Flexible groups are never permanent. They are dissolved once the goals of the learning activity are met. Three types of groups provide opportunities for learners to take a more active role in learning.

In teacher-led groups, whether whole class or small group, the teacher articulates the goal of the activity, paces and leads the interaction, models appropriate responses, and provides timely feedback. The goal of the teacher-led group is to actively engage all learners to solve a specific problem or offer explanations, perspectives, or points of view. Active participation is a must.

In collaborative learning groups, students take responsibility for directing the activities of the group. Students must work together to publicly share ideas, gather information, assign work tasks, and plan and produce, a product that reflects a contribution by all group members. Each collaborative learning group should include a wide range of student abilities; their purpose is to pool their resources to demonstrate knowledge and understanding of a particular subject or topic.

Performance-based groups by comparison are formed to align the challenge level of the learning task with the demonstrated abilities of students in the group. Each group is organized to solve a specific problem, answer a challenging question, model a suggested procedure, or complete an application task related to recent learning. In performance-based groups, the teacher's role is to match the demands of the learning activity with the upper limits of the group's potential, monitor student engagement, and provide feedback and support. Ideally students in performance-based groups would select a problem or a learning activity that their group would like to try and then work together to complete the assigned task.

It is the supreme art of the teacher to awaken joy in creative expression and knowledge.

—Albert Einstein

Reports from teachers in the field confirm that informally grouping and regrouping students in a variety of ways makes a teacher's job easier and students more productive. Experts on grouping include Robert Slavin and Roger and David Johnson. The work of Merrill Harmin and Doug Buehl also contains tested practices for increasing active student engagement with subject matter.

How do teachers in our school help students become producers of knowledge once the acquisition phase of learning is complete?

What do teachers in our school do to encourage students to become self-directed learners?

How do teachers in our school encourage students to self-assess their performances?

LOOKING DEEPER

WHAT DO YOU SEE IN CLASSROOMS WHERE LEARNING PERFORMANCES ARE NONNEGOTIABLE COMPONENTS OF CLASSROOM TEACHING?

Place a check indicating an aspect of your school program that is particularly effective.

LEARNER PERFORMANCE IN CLASSROOMS: PRODUCTS, ACTIVITIES, AND ARTIFACTS

___ *Alternative assessments*

___ *Applying information in different contexts*

___ *Building concrete models*

___ *Case studies*

___ *Contests/competitions*

___ *Data gathering*

___ *Debates*

___ *Dramatizations*

___ *Experiments*

___ *Field trips*

___ *Games*

___ *Giving reports*

___ *Group work*

___ *Guided practice activities*

___ *Interactive CDs*

___ *Internet projectors*

___ *Making slides/movies*

___ *Making things work*

___ *Manipulation activities*

___ *Model making*

___ *Movement activities*

___ *Portfolios*

___ *PowerPoint presentations*

Notes:

Discuss evidence of your assessment.

___ Presentations

___ Problem-finding activities

___ Problem-solving activities

___ Project work

___ Puzzles

___ Research projects

___ Rubrics

___ Self-testing activities

___ Skills demonstrations

___ Sports activities

___ Step-by-step procedures

___ Survey activities

___ Technical writing

___ Technology use

___ Unit tests

___ Video experiments

___ Weekly tests

___ Work centers

___ Worksheets for mastery

___ Writing journals

Notes:

Discuss evidence of your assessment.

THE PEDAGOGY OF LEARNER PERFORMANCE
(what the teacher must accomplish)

___ Demonstrate and model correct process

___ Guide student practice

___ Provide feedback/encouragement

___ Engage students in problem-solving and solution-finding
activities

___ Encourage students to take ownership of their learning

___ Build on student success/manage limitations

___ Group students for success

Notes:

Discuss evidence of your assessment.

THE VERBS OF LEARNER PERFORMANCE IN ACTION
(what the kids are doing)

__ Adapting	__ Labeling
__ Adjusting	__ Measuring
__ Answering	__ Organizing
__ Calculating	__ Ordering
__ Completing	__ Predicting
__ Conducting	__ Presenting
__ Converting	__ Ranking
__ Deciding	__ Recording
__ Demonstrating	__ Revising
__ Developing	__ Self-checking
__ Documenting	__ Selecting
__ Dramatizing	__ Showing
__ Drawing	__ Simulating
__ Exploring	__ Solving
__ Formulating	__ Specifying
__ Giving examples	__ Teaching
__ Illustrating	__ Testing
__ Incorporating	__ Tracing
__ Investigating	__ Writing
__ Justifying	

Notes:

Discuss evidence of your assessment.

TAKING ACTION

TASK ONE: WALK-THRU

Directions: Complete several Performance Phase Walk-Thru templates to get a sense of how teachers in your school promote active learning.

See Figure 9.1

First Note: What Works Now:
_____
_____
_____
_____

Then list specific barriers to incorporating Student
Performance in classroom:

_____
_____
_____
_____

TASK TWO: PERFORMANCE RUBRIC

Directions: Complete the Performance Rubric below and informally discuss your assessment with colleagues.
Based upon recent observations, the following is appropriate:

- Celebrate and recognize exemplary student performance use throughout the school

- Organize faculty study group teams to support experimentation with performance strategies in classrooms

- Ask for assistance on performance use from district-level support professionals

- Other

See Figure 9.2

CLASSROOM WALK-THRU

PERFORMANCE: SUPPORTING LEARNER PERFORMANCE

CONTENT TAUGHT _____

_____

DATE _____

IDENTIFYING KEY CONCEPTS

- DEMONSTRATE/MODEL APPLICATIONS
- GUIDE STUDENT PRACTICE (INDIVIDUAL/GROUP)
- PROVIDE FEEDBACK/ENCOURAGEMENT
- ENGAGE STUDENTS IN PROBLEM SOLVING/SELF-TESTING
- ENCOURAGE STUDENTS TO DEMONSTRATE MASTERY/ABILITY
- BUILD ON STUDENT SUCCESS/MANAGE LIMITATIONS

INSIGHTS NOTED:

ACTIVITIES/RESOURCES

- GUIDED PRACTICE ACTIVITIES
- PROJECT WORK
- EXPERIMENTS
- DEMONSTRATIONS
- LEARNING CHALLENGES
- STUDY GROUPS/SELF-TESTING
- FORMAL TESTING
- TECHNOLOGY
- TUTORING ACTIVITIES
- COMPACTING
- RUBRICS
- DRAMATIZATIONS
- MANIPULATIONS
- OTHER

ACTIVITIES/RESOURCES OBSERVED:

NOTE WELL: This Walk-Thru is intended to promote shared meaning about best practice in teaching; it should never be used to evaluate teacher performance.

Figure 9.1

PERFORMANCE RUBRIC

GUIDING LEARNER PERFORMANCE

Check the appropriate level of implementation.

Supporting relevant practice, experimentation, and self-testing.

GUIDING PRINCIPLE:
In classrooms where students work together and individually to create products, reconstruct and apply new learning in a variety of ways and test their level of understanding performance is enhanced.

1 Teachers in our school rarely use flexible grouping and guided practice techniques to deepen student learning.

2 Teachers in our school sometimes use flexible grouping and guided practice techniques to deepen student learning.

3 Teachers in our school often use flexible grouping and guided practice techniques to deepen student learning.

4 Teachers in our school always use flexible grouping and guided practice techniques to deepen student learning.

Reliable Indicators:

- Guided Practice Activities
- Flexible learning groups
- Formative assessments and rubric use
- Modeling of correct process
- Learning Buzz / Collaborative Learning
- Monitoring student progress and performance
- Peer assessment / refinement
- Technology support in use

Figure 9.2

TASK THREE: SHARE FAIR MONTH – WEEK THREE

Group teachers into voluntary pairs or triads and ask them to discuss the Performance Phase of Mindful Teaching and share success stories and offer each other suggestions about how to better prepare students for meaningful learning.

FIRST: **Designate Week Three of Share Fair month to the Performance Phase of Mindful Teaching.**

NOW: **Ask teachers to collect classroom examples of Performance Phase activities and resources.**

FINALLY: **Hold periodic meetings for teachers to explain and share these ideas and resources.** These meetings can be organized as follows:
- By departments
- By teaching teams
- By nonteaching periods
- By grade levels
- By subject area
- By interest
- By faculty

Note: In the third week of Share Fair, it is very important to connect resources and activities to the following:
- *Affirming understanding*
- *Applying information in different contexts*
- *Assessing for mastery*

Remember each phase of Mindful Teaching will have its own week.

MAKING SENSE

THE VOCABULARY OF LEARNER PERFORMANCE

ALTERNATIVE ASSESSMENTS

are measures of a student's knowledge or ability, other than standardized tests, in which the student originates a response to a task or question.

APPLICATION

is putting into practice abstract learning and applying concepts in concrete situations. For application tasks, students complete real or simulated tasks using the content in ways that evidence their level of understanding, such as providing written evidence of knowledge, testing ideas for unique applications, building replications and representations of ideas, conducting experiments, and/or demonstrating skills.

CLASS MEETINGS

are gatherings of a class for the purpose of emphasizing the relevance of subject matter and social problem solving. Popularized for use in schools by William Glasser, there are three kinds of class meetings: (1) the problem-solving meeting to solve social and behavioral problems, (2) the open-ended meeting to deal with academic matters, and (3) the educational-diagnostic meeting to find out how well students understand the concepts of the curriculum.

COLLABORATIVE LEARNING

is group learning designed to teach students to work together toward a common goal. Working in collaborative groups, students share ideas, gather information, assign work tasks, and plan and produce a product that reflects a contribution by all group members. The purpose of collaborative learning is to teach students how to work together, share ideas, organize information, delegate assigned tasks, and manage time.

EMPATHY

is identification with or sharing of another's feelings, situation, or attitudes; the attribution of one's personal feelings or attitudes to an external object.

To be wholly devoted to some intellectual exercise is to have succeeded in life.

—Robert Louis Stevenson

Successful teachers are surpassed by their pupils.

—Anonymous

EXPLANATION

is a statement that makes something comprehensible by describing the relevant structure, operation, or circumstances. For explanation tasks, students generate examples that help explain the key ideas in the content, grapple with essential questions, share understandings, and explain how they would solve problems.

GUIDED PRACTICE

engages groups of students in working through problems that use subject matter knowledge. The guidance comes partly from an organized pattern of problem solving that highlights identifying the problem, gathering information, and generating and evaluating candidate solutions.

In guided practice activities, teachers give students learning tasks that challenge their ability to solve problems, find solutions, and build a better mousetrap. Guided means that the teacher is ever vigilant to guarantee purposeful application and provide "in progress" feedback. Practice means that these are application tasks that become increasingly more complex as the learner gains expertise through repeated practice.

INTERPRETATION

is a mental representation of the meaning or significance of something. For interpretation tasks, students create and share a coherent, interesting account (or story) of the content, making sense of the facts, pointing out examples from other sources, and giving a personal interpretation of their present level of understanding.

PERSPECTIVE

is the appearance of things relative to one another as determined by their distance from the viewer. Perspective is a way of placing ideas in context to generate insightful, plausible assumptions.

PORTFOLIOS

are collections of student work representing a selection of performance. Portfolios in classrooms are derived from the visual and performing arts tradition in which they serve to showcase artists' accomplishments and personally favored works. A portfolio may be a folder containing a student's best pieces and the student's evaluation of the strengths and weaknesses of the pieces. It may also contain one or more works in progress that illustrate the creation of a product, such as an essay, evolving through various stages of conception, drafting, and revision.

RUBRICS

are criteria used to assess and communicate student performance with regard to specific aspects of learning. Rubric refers to a graphic scoring grid designed to communicate and assess levels of performance. Usually written in chart or table formats, rubrics provide objective criteria students can use to determine where they are in pursuit of some standard of excellence.

SELF-ASSESSMENT

is a way to uncover personal skills, abilities and interests. Self-assessment is the classification of oneself with respect to worth.

SELF-DIRECTED LEARNING

is the ability to motivate oneself to solve problems and to monitor one's own progress. Self-directed learners think about what they are doing while they are doing it.

SELF-KNOWLEDGE

is knowledge of one's self, or of one's own character, powers, and limitations. Self-knowledge enables learners to self-assess and self-regulate understandings in order to advance them.

LOOKING WIDER

SUGGESTED READINGS

Buehl, Doug, "Classroom Strategies for Interactive Learning," International Reading Association, Inc., 2001

Glasser, William, "Schools Without Failure," HarperCollins Publishers, Inc., 1975

Harmin, Merrill, "Inspiring Active Learning," Association for Supervision and Curriculum Development, 1994

Jensen, Eric, "Brain-Based Learning," Corwin Press, 2000

Johnson, David W., and Johnson, Roger T., "Meaningful Assessment: A Manageable and Cooperative Process," Allyn & Bacon, 2001

Newmann, F., Marks, H., and Gamoran, A., "Authentic Pedagogy," Standards That Boost Student Performance. Issues in Restructuring Schools, Report No. 8, Center on Organization and Restructuring Schools, 1995

Slavin, R., and Fashola, O., "Show Me the Evidence: Proven and Promising Programs for America's Schools," Corwin Press, 1998

Sousa, David A., "How the Brain Works," The National Association of Secondary School Principals, 1995

Stiggins, R., "Student-Involved Classroom Assessment (3rd ed.), Prentice Hall, 2001

Tomlinson, Carol Ann, "The Differentiated Classroom," The Institute for Evidence-Based Decision-Making in Education, Inc., 2000

Wiggins, Grant, and McTighe, Jay, "Understanding by Design," The Institute for Evidence-Based Decision-Making in Education, Inc., 1998

SIGNS OF SUCCESS WORTH FIGHTING FOR

- *Frequent use of performance assessments*
- *Emphasis on student-generated products*
- *Displayed student work*
- *Group assignments*
- *Use of technology to support learning beyond the textbook*
- *Flexible grouping practices*

*Learning is not all
in your head.*

—Carla Hannaford

LINKING STUDENT PERFORMANCE LEARNING

DIRECTIONS

Generate and share a suggested list of resources on classroom activities that
teachers can use to enhance student self-directed learning.

CREATING A LEARNING PLACE

PERSONAL REFLECTIONS:

Jot down your main learnings from Chapter 9

CHAPTER TEN: AFFIRMING STUDENT UNDERSTANDING

ESSENTIAL QUESTION:
What can classroom teachers do to affirm and validate student learning?

BIG IDEA — KNOWLEDGE IS GENERATIVE; IT MAKES ROOM FOR NEW GROWTH.

Have you ever wondered why seemingly average students seem to struggle with even simple learning tasks? The answer to this question lies in the history of the learner. For many learners, the exhilarating feeling that accompanies learning a difficult idea is not part of their schooling experience or more likely is not a feeling that is even recognizable to them.

I have come to feel that the only learning that significantly influences behavior is self-discovered, self-appropriated learning.

—Carl Rogers

LEARNING IS NEVER COMPLETE WITHOUT THE FEELING OF HAVING ACCOMPLISHED SOMETHING CHALLENGING.

The Transfer Phase of Mindful Teaching is all about helping students experience that exhilarating feeling of accomplishment that comes with learning something challenging. Transfer is when what has been learned gets "turned over." It's when the youngster who first learns to ride a bike takes off and pops a "wheelie." It is when all of the ideas, experiences, and performances that the teacher so carefully mediated in Readiness, Delivery, and Performance are expressed as a change in the learner's capacity to know, act on, and think about ideas in the future.

MINDSHIFT: *Experiencing the exhilarating power of learning makes the difficulties sustainable.*

In the Transfer Phase of Mindful Teaching, students take ownership of what has been learned and reflect, integrate, and share their unique interpretations with others.

In the Transfer Phase of Mindful Teaching, students test new applications in action.

In the Transfer Phase of Mindful Teaching, purposeful reflection, self-testing, self-monitoring, writing, new questions, insightful thinking, and integrative expressions rule.

In the Transfer Phase of Mindful Teaching, the awareness of self-change and the evaluation of individual progress are major goals.

Transfer as it is intended here is that phase of learning that stretches a student's mind around ideas in ways that give rise to new levels of competence.

LOOKING DEEPER

WHAT DO YOU SEE IN CLASSROOMS WHERE THE TRANSFER PHASE OF LEARNING IS A NONNEGOTIABLE COMPONENT OF CLASSROOM TEACHING?

Place a check indicating an aspect of your school program that is particularly effective.

LOOKING IN CLASSROOMS: PRODUCTS, ACTIVITIES, AND ARTIFACTS

__ *Creative art*	__ *Research papers*
__ *Creative writing*	__ *Reports*
__ *Debates*	__ *Rubrics*
__ *Displays of work*	__ *Self-evaluation*
__ *Exhibits*	__ *Service projects*
__ *Exit slips*	__ *Simulations*
__ *Expressive papers/brochures*	__ *Songs*
__ *Inventions*	__ *Storyboards*
__ *Journals*	__ *Student writing*
__ *Mock interviews*	__ *Speeches*
__ *Pattern visuals*	__ *Testing*
__ *Peer edits*	__ *Teaching each other*
__ *Performances*	__ *Time for reflective thinking*
__ *Photo essays*	__ *Unit tests*
__ *Portfolios*	__ *Video projects*
__ *Presentations*	__ *Weekly tests*
__ *Projects*	

Notes:

Discuss evidence of your assessment.

THE VERBS OF ASSESSMENT AND TRANSFER

(what the kids are doing)

__ Adapting

__ Constructing new knowledge

__ Critiquing

__ Defending

__ Evaluating

__ Explaining new perspectives

__ Expressing (journals)

__ Formulating

__ Illustrating

__ Modifying

__ Performing

__ Predicting

__ Refuting

__ Relearning

__ Restating

__ Reconstructing

__ Reflective thinking

__ Self-testing

__ Summarizing

__ Synthesizing

__ Teaching others

__ Translating

__ Transmitting

__ Uncovering

__ Verifying

__ Writing

Notes:

Discuss evidence of your assessment.

THE PEDAGOGY FOR TRANSFER

(what the teacher must accomplish)

__ Consolidate and integrate new learning

__ Assess student knowledge, skills, and abilities and provide feedback

__ Facilitate multiple expressions/representations of new learning

__ Generate new questions and applications of new learning

__ Guide student reflection and writing

__ Move students to insightful thinking

__ Evaluate the relevance of new learning

Notes:

Discuss evidence of your assessment.

TAKING ACTION

TRANSFER OF LEARNING

Looking in classrooms: Reflect upon your teaching practice and then visit several classrooms to look for classroom activities and products that you can use to enhance transfer of learning.

What are the existing strengths of your school with regard to the Transfer Phase of teaching?

TRANSFER NOTES:

TASK ONE: WALK-THRU

Directions: Complete several Transfer Phase Walk-Thru templates to get a sense of how teachers in your school promote active learning.

See Figure 10.1

First Note: What Works Now:

_____

_____

_____

_____

Then list specific barriers to incorporating Transfer Activities in classroom:

_____

_____

_____

TASK TWO: TRANSFER ACTION ITEMS

Based upon recent observations, the following is appropriate:

- Celebrate and recognize exemplary transfer activities throughout the school

- Organize faculty study-group teams to support experimentation with transfer activities in classrooms

- Ask for assistance on transfer activities from district-level support professionals

- Other

See Figure 10.2

CLASSROOM WALK-THRU

TRANSFER: PROMOTING LEARNER EXPRESSION AND INSIGHT

CONTENT TAUGHT _____

_____

DATE _____

IDENTIFYING KEY CONCEPTS

- GUIDING MULTIPLE REPRESENTATIONS OF CONTENT
- GENERATING NEW QUESTIONS
- GUIDING STUDENT REFLECTION AND WRITING
- HELPING STUDENTS CONSOLIDATE AND INTEGRATE NEW LEARNING
- MOVING STUDENTS TO PERSONAL INSIGHTS

INSIGHTS NOTED:

ACTIVITIES/RESOURCES

- PORTFOLIO PROJECTS
- WRITING: PERSONAL, FORMAL, PROCEDURAL, CREATIVE
- PEER EDITING
- PERFORMANCE/DEMONSTRATION
- DISPLAY OF QUALITY WORK
- CRITIQUES
- CASE STUDIES

ACTIVITIES/RESOURCES OBSERVED:

NOTE WELL: This Walk-Thru is intended to promote shared meaning about best practice in teaching; it should never be used to evaluate teacher performance.

Figure 10.1

TRANSFER RUBRIC

TEACHING TRANSFER

Promoting insight, construction of knowledge, creativity, unique applications, and social responsibility in classrooms.

Check the appropriate level of implementation.

GUIDING PRINCIPLE:

In classrooms where students are challenged to refine, evaluate, and synthesize new learning, transfer of learning is enhanced.

1

Teachers in our school rarely use the transfer strategies described in this chapter.

2

Teachers in our school sometimes use the transfer strategies described in this chapter.

3

Teachers in our school often use the transfer strategies described in this chapter.

4

Teachers in our school always use the transfer strategies described in this chapter.

Reliable Indicators:

- Incentives for creative representation of content learned
- Perspective taking and real-world applications of new learning
- Extensive use of writing and documentation of understanding
- Quality student work displayed
- Self-testing and relearning
- Encouragement of insightful applications of content learned

Figure 10.2

TAKING ACTION

TASK THREE: SHARE FAIR MONTH – WEEK FOUR

Group teachers into voluntary pairs or triads and ask them to discuss the Transfer Phase of Mindful Teaching and share success stories and offer each other suggestions about how to better prepare students for meaningful learning.

FIRST: Designate Week Four of Share Fair month to the Transfer Phase of Mindful Teaching.

NOW: Ask teachers to collect classroom examples of Transfer Phase activities and resources.

FINALLY: Hold periodic meetings for teachers to explain and share these ideas and resources. These meetings can be organized as follows:
- By departments
- By teaching teams
- By nonteaching periods
- By grade levels
- By subject area
- By interest
- By faculty

Note: In the fourth week of Share Fair, it is very important to connect resources and activities to the following:
- *Consolidating new learning*
- *Creating multiple expressions of subject matter*
- *Engaging learners in insightful thinking, writing, and reflecting*

Remember each phase of Mindful Teaching will have its own week.

MAKING SENSE

THE VOCABULARY OF LEARNING TRANSFER

ALTERNATIVE ASSESSMENTS

are forms of measuring a student's knowledge or ability other than standardized tests in which students originate a response to a task or question.

FORMATIVE ASSESSMENT

takes place during the course of teaching. It provides information to teachers and students about the kind of learning that is taking place in order to improve learning. It provides information for teachers to use in discussing progress with pupils in planning appropriate next steps in learning. In the Transfer Phase of Mindful Teaching formative assessments provide timely feedback related to quality and development of transfer activities.

INTEGRATIVE EXPRESSIONS

are expressions that tend to combine and coordinate diverse elements into a whole.

INTERPRETATION

is a mental representation of the meaning or significance of something. For interpretation tasks, students create and share a coherent, interesting account (or story) of the content, making sense of the facts, pointing out examples from other sources, and giving a personal interpretation of their present level of understanding.

MOCK INTERVIEWS

are simulated interviews, designed to develop or test the communication skills of the interviewees.

PERSPECTIVE

is the appearance of things relative to one another as determined by their distance from the viewer. Perspective is a way of regarding situations or topics, etc. In the Transfer Phase of Mindful Teaching, the learner's perspective is nonnegotiable.

PORTFOLIOS

are collections of student work representing a selection of performance. Portfolios in classrooms today are derived from the visual and performing arts tradition in which they serve to showcase artists' accomplishments and personally favored works. A portfolio may be a folder containing a student's best pieces and the student's evaluation of the strengths and weaknesses of the pieces. It may also contain one or more works in progress that illustrate the creation of a product, such as an essay, evolving through various stages of conception, drafting, and revision.

PURPOSEFUL REFLECTION

is intent consideration that transforms the materials of classes, work, and other projects into something that you make yourself, ongoing and dynamically, so that your curriculum belongs to you. Purposeful reflection coupled with formal, student-generated expression is the work of the Transfer Phase of Mindful Teaching.

REFUTING

is disproving and overthrowing by argument, evidence, or countervailing proof; proving to be false or erroneous.

RUBRICS

are authoritative rules of conduct or procedure. Rubric refers to a graphic scoring grid designed to communicate and assess levels of performance. Rubrics give students objective criteria they can use to determine where they are in pursuit of some standard of excellence.

SELF-ASSESSMENT

is a way to uncover skills, values, and interests. Self-assessment is the classification of oneself with respect to worth.

SELF-DIRECTED LEARNING

is the ability to motivate oneself to solve problems and to monitor one's own progress. Self-directed learners think about what they are doing while doing it.

SELF-KNOWLEDGE

is knowledge of one's self, or of one's own character, powers, limitations, etc. Self-knowledge is an understanding of oneself and one's goals and abilities.

SUMMATIVE ASSESSMENT

reports the overall achievement of students at the end of a course of study:

- Takes place at certain intervals
- Relates to progression in learning against public criteria
- Produces results for both individuals and groups of pupils
- Requires methods that are as reliable as possible
- Involves some quality assurance procedures
- Should be based on evidence from the full range of performance relevant to the criteria being used
- Is used to provide information about how much students have learned and how well a course has worked

TAKING ACTION

TASK ONE: WALK-THRU

Complete several Walk-Thru templates to get a sense of what the Transfer Phase of Mindful Teaching looks like in action.

Remember a Walk-Thru is not a formal observation. It has nothing to do with the evaluation of teaching. The goal of the Walk-Thru is to increase shared meanings among faculty members about what good teaching looks like in different contexts. Walk-Thrus are designed to be completed in a very short period of time, even in passing.

TASK TWO: LESSON PLANNER AND UNIT GUIDE

Review the following Unit Planning Guide and Lesson Planner in department or grade-level meetings. These templates are designed to help teachers integrate aspects of Mindful Teaching into their existing classroom routines.

One option for adapting the Unit Planning Guide to your particular situation is to use it to chronicle a unit of instruction that you have already taught. By reconstructing the teaching activities of a previously taught unit by allocation of time and activity in each of the four phases, teachers can begin to make decisions about specific areas of teaching they might improve. The Lesson Planner template can be used similarly. See Figures 10.3 and 10.4.

TASK THREE: SHARING BEST PRACTICE IN CLASSROOM TEACHING

Schedule a faculty retreat or conference on Best Practice in Teaching and have department chairpersons give group presentations about their department's observations of Mindful Teaching Practices.

UNIT PLANNING GUIDE

CONTENT _____ DURATION _____

| INSTRUCTIONAL ACTIVITIES | | RESOURCES/REFERENCES |

STANDARDS/BENCHMARKS

STUDENTS WILL:

-
-
-
-
-
-
-
-

READINESS

DELIVERY

PERFORMANCE

TRANSFER

Figure 10.3
Page 1

UNIT PLANNING GUIDE

ESSENTIAL QUESTIONS	ASSESSMENTS
1.	
2.	
3.	
4.	
5.	
6.	
7.	

Figure 10.3
Page 2

LESSON PLANNER

LESSON _____ DATE _____

CONTENT TARGETS/BIG IDEAS	TIME	WHAT THE TEACHER DOES	WHAT THE STUDENT DOES
STANDARDS	OPEN		
	LESSON		**ASSESSMENT**
INSTRUCTION SET OPTIONS			

INSTRUCTION SET OPTIONS
- Activate Interest
- Connect to Prior Knowledge
- Communicate Expectations
- Frame the Content
- Exchange Ideas/Lecture
- Probe with Questions
- Affirm Understanding
- Apply/Guided Practice
- Assess/Perform
- Validate/Reinforce Success
- Other: _____

CLOSE

Figure 10.4

LOOKING WIDER

SUGGESTED READINGS

Buzan, Tony, and Buzan, Barry, "The Mind Map Book," BBC Books, 1993

Marzano, Robert J., "What Works in Schools," Association for Supervision and Curriculum Development, 2003

Cotton, Kathleen, Northwest Regional Educational Laboratory, "Research You Can Use to Improve Results," Association for Supervision and Curriculum Development, 1995

White, Richard, and Gunstone, Richard, "Probing Understanding," The Falmer Press, 1992

SIGNS OF SUCCESS WORTH FIGHTING FOR

- *Incorporation of student self-testing practices in classrooms*
- *Integrated writing projects emphasizing perspective taking and insightful thinking*
- *Artistic and/or creative expressions of content learned*
- *Self-directed student learning projects*
- *Affirmation of student progress*
- *Journals in use*

If true understanding has been gained, we will be able to make plans and develop new ideas about what that experience implies for our future.

—James Zull

WHAT SPECIFIC STUDENT PERFORMANCES GIVE EVIDENCE OF A SUCCESSFUL LEARNING EXPERIENCE?

The ability to:

CREATING A LEARNING PLACE

PERSONAL REFLECTIONS:

Jot down your main learnings from Chapter 10

CHAPTER ELEVEN: SUPPORTING PROFESSIONAL DEVELOPMENT

ESSENTIAL QUESTION:
How can we orchestrate student and teacher development simultaneously?

BIG IDEA — THE PROFESSIONAL DEVELOPMENT OF TEACHERS IS A MEANS RATHER THAN AN END.

Having gifts that differ according to the grace given to us, let us use them.
— Romans 12: 4—6

We hope that by now you agree that the physical, organizational, and social contexts of your school have deep and lasting effects upon student learning. Our message has been that successful schools get results because they are adaptive in ways that cannot be fully prescribed externally or in advance. In other words, learning places constantly reorganize themselves in ways that are more responsive to the specific needs of their students. Patterns of behavior, like the respectful connections between people, increased access to learning for students who would otherwise go unnoticed, and always having a learning response for new challenges are big things to these schools.

Although not often treated as such, learning programs for teachers is another powerful context of an adaptive, responsive Learning Place. Where schools make a commitment to provide job-embedded time for teachers to convert new knowledge into classrooms practices, school improvement is virtually guaranteed.

Professional learning is a team sport.
— Anonymous

The traditional point of view is that teachers belong in classrooms while administrators run the school. Unfortunately, this point of view is alive and well in many communities and makes it difficult to allocate noninstructional time for professional development. Until the school community can be convinced of the benefits of involving classroom teachers in ongoing, focused inquiry and collaborative problem solving, mediocrity will carry the day. Thus schools that succeed in orchestrating teacher and student development simultaneously increase, by double, their chances of creating a professional learning community.

It is essential for each and every teacher to continue to learn what they can about improving teaching and the school; but for this to occur, there must be a shared commitment to provide time and resources at the school level and support for the Professional Development of teachers in the community at large. As communities of learners, teachers are more likely to develop and pursue: shared missions, collaborative teams, action orientations, collective inquiry initiatives, continuous improvement, and results (DuFour, 2005).

In other words, Learning Places are "in progress" prototypes of Professional Learning Communities. They are incubators of events, causes, ideas, and objects aimed at creating schools that provide quality education for all students. They are places where teachers, students, and parents come together regularly to learn from each other.

It is crucial to avoid thinking of Professional Development as capacity-building activities that only occur within the school. The scope of Professional Development is wider than an individual school. It begins there, but for it to be sustained, it must be connected to a larger infrastructure such as a league of schools, cohorts of sister schools, a school district, or a learning consortium. A good case in point is our work in York Region, a large multicultural school district just north of Toronto (see Sharratt & Fullan, 2006). York has approximately 170 schools. In 2001, we began to work with the district to improve literacy across the district. The main strategy involved linking a community of schools with a focus on literacy improvement (it is critical to note that Professional Development initiatives must always have an obvious instructional focus—Learning Places are not just about diffuse interaction).

We started in September 2002, with teams from 40 elementary schools. Each team consisted of the principal (always the principal), the lead literacy teacher, and the special education resource teacher. In 2003, we added 65 schools, including several secondary schools that wanted to Develop Professional Learning Communities. In 2004, all remaining schools joined, including all the high schools. We have the entire district working on improving literacy as the main vehicle for reform. The content of this work consists of implementing 13 components of a literacy strategy, using data to drive instruction, enabling teachers to learn from each other within the school, facilitating schools to learn from each other (lateral capacity building), developing leadership capacity of principals and teacher leaders, and so on.

The results are impressive. York Region is now showing strong achievement results on the Ontario Provincial Tests in reading, writing, and math; deeper analysis shows that those schools most thoroughly implementing the new culture are getting even greater results. Current efforts are directed at supporting the development of 33 schools (27 elementary and 6 high schools) that have the farthest to go, while working with all schools to keep the momentum going.

What happens when the whole system works on Developing Learning Places is not only that knowledge flows, but also the process creates social cohesion and collective commitment among participants. In this context, both knowledge and moral purpose provide the energy for going to new levels of achievement.

You may not be in a district like York Region. Your effort may be directed inside one school. But our strong advice is that you figure out how you can learn from other schools and also contribute to the learning of other schools. This strengthens individual schools as well as the district. Otherwise your gains will be fragile.

GETTING STARTED

GETTING STARTED

How does our school publicize the purposes and benefits of regularly scheduled Professional Development activities?

GETTING STARTED

How does our school make time for teachers to convert new knowledge about teaching and learning into schoolwide and classroom practices?

GETTING STARTED

How can we network our Professional Development initiatives with "sister schools" to exchange ideas and resources?

Individual schools can become highly collaborative despite the district they are in, but cannot stay highly collaborative despite the district.

LOOKING DEEPER

WHAT DO YOU SEE IN SCHOOLS WHERE TEACHER LEARNING AND PROFESSIONAL DEVELOPMENT ARE PRIORITIES?

Place a check indicating an aspect of your school program that is particularly effective.

Learning Places.

__ *Action research*

__ *Brochures about professional development projects*

__ *Collaborative teaching projects*

__ *Exchange teacher programs with other schools*

__ *Faculty retreats*

__ *Guest lectures from local colleges and universities*

__ *High levels of teacher efficacy*

__ *Individual teacher learning projects*

__ *Informal "in-house" publications on quality teaching*

__ *Ongoing affiliation with local universities*

__ *Opportunities for distance learning at school*

__ *Opportunities for teachers to observe colleagues*

__ *Professional libraries*

__ *Professional organization affiliations*

__ *Professional resource collections*

__ *Publications to parents about staff development activities*

__ *Recognition for excellence in teaching*

__ *Research summaries*

__ *Shared teaching materials and resources*

__ *Shared, participatory leadership*

__ *Study groups*

__ *Teacher learning clusters*

__ *Teacher subject matter networks*

__ *Teachers applying for fellowships and learning grants*

__ *Teachers searching the literature on teaching*

__ *Teachers visiting other schools*

__ *Technology resources dedicated to professional learning*

__ *Visiting professors and teachers*

Notes:

Discuss evidence of your assessment.

COLLABORATIVE PLANNING

___ *Acceptance of complexity*

___ *Active leadership participation in professional development initiatives*

___ *Active study groups*

___ *An atmosphere of openness*

___ *Creative problem-solving sessions*

___ *Faculty support for continuous development*

___ *High growth expectation*

___ *Multiple approaches to professional learning*

___ *No "non-discussables"*

___ *Pragmatic approaches to barriers to success*

___ *Professional reading groups*

___ *Shared decision making*

___ *Teachers sharing new books, articles, and teaching material*

___ *Time and resources formally allocated for professional development*

> Notes:
>
>
>
> *Discuss evidence of your assessment.*

EXPERIMENTATION

___ *"In-progress" assessments of new programs*

___ *Bulletin boards labeled "New Teaching Ideas"*

___ *Emphasis upon experimentation*

___ *Publications explaining innovations*

___ *Reports and results documentation*

___ *Study groups*

Life has meaning when we have a purpose that justifies our strivings...

—— Mihaly Csikszentmihalyi

> Notes:
>
>
>
> *Discuss evidence of your assessment.*

LOOKING FOR EVIDENCE THAT PROFESSIONAL DEVELOPMENT IS VALUED

Using the descriptors listed above, on a scale of 1–10, how does your school rate as a place where Teacher Learning and Professional Development are valued? Explain your assessment.

1	2	3	4	5	6	7	8	9	10

SUPPORT YOUR ASSESSMENT

TAKING ACTION

Directions: Form an "Action Team" of parents and teachers to investigate attitudes about the benefits of involving teachers in sustained inquiry and school improvement initiatives as part of their regular schedule.

TASK ONE: SURVEY PARENTS AND SCHEDULE A FORUM

- Create a survey to determine parent beliefs about the benefits of allocating noninstructional time for teacher learning, collaboration, and problem solving.
- Distribute the survey to interested parents and involved community members.
- Tabulate results and create a plan to build support for job-embedded professional development programs to include the following:
- Write and publish a handout/brochure on the topic that:

    1. Describes the rationale for allocating time for the professional development of teachers.
    2. Identifies existing forms of professional development presently sanctioned for use by schools in the district.
    3. Cites research that links teacher professional development to improvements in student learning and organizational improvement in the school.
    4. Invites parents to participate in a community forum on the subject.

- At the forum, briefly discuss results of the survey and implications for future action.
- Invite interested teachers to speak about innovations in classroom teaching that require coordination and planning before they can be implemented.
- End the meeting with a vision statement about the school's goals for future development.

A sample survey created by the National Staff Development Council is available at www.nsdc.org/library/policy/SDLCCharts.pdf

TASK TWO: REORGANIZING TIME

Review the existing literature to generate options for creating time and a relevant framework for professional development activities.

Compile a summary of this information and submit your report for consideration by the faculty.

(The Time Dilemma in School Restructuring *by Gary Watts and Shari Castle is an excellent source; see also the National Staff Development Council and Association for Supervision and Curriculum Development websites for relevant publications and products.*)

TASK THREE: PROFESSIONAL DEVELOPMENT INITIATIVE

Plan and implement at least one professional development initiative this school year.

We live in a time of such rapid change and growth of knowledge that only he who is in a fundamental sense a scholar — that is, a person who continues to learn and inquire — can hope to keep pace, let alone play the role of guide.

—Nathan M. Pusey

VOLUNTARY ACTION ITEM

Select those descriptors you consider essential to the Professional Development of teachers and design a "Learning Together" brochure that visitors can use to focus attention on the instructional goals of your Professional Development initiatives. Remember to document your school's accomplishments in this area. Note: A published schedule of the Professional Development activities will go a long way toward gaining public support for the continued development of teachers in your school.

This visual representation will help make your school's existing potential both public and visible. It will also create new energy needed to move to action.

We are wiser than we know.

—Ralph Waldo Emerson

WHAT TO LOOK FOR

MAKING SENSE

THE VOCABULARY OF PROFESSIONAL DEVELOPMENT

ACCEPTANCE OF COMPLEXITY

is the awareness that school reform rarely unfolds as intended.
Creating highly functioning schools is more a matter of searching for
patterns of interaction that ensure collaboration around ideas that have
a basis in informed literature and show promise as a practical solution
to the specific needs of the school. This is no simple task and should
not be treated as such.

ACTION RESEARCH

is an internal inquiry process that invites teachers to experiment with new
ideas and ways of teaching. Less formal than other forms of research,
action research is a trial and error process of searching for a best fit
between a specific group of students and educational innovations.

EFFICACY

is generally defined as the power to cause a desired effect. In schools,
efficacy is used to describe individual teacher beliefs that confirm that
quality-schooling practices have real and lasting effects upon learners.

FACULTY RETREATS

are organized professional development programs designed to provide a
school faculty with a fresh set of perspectives for deepening their
commitment to improve opportunities for learning for their students
and the school community.

ONGOING CRITICAL INQUIRY

is a commitment to challenge existing structures for teaching and
learning by regularly experimenting with different ways to organize
and manage the schooling process.

PARTICIPATORY LEADERSHIP

is an organizational practice that brings together people who have a
shared purpose, a common knowledge base, and specific vocabulary to
work together to solve a problem or decide upon a course of action.

*The world of knowledge
takes a crazy turn when
teachers themselves are
taught to learn.*

—Bertolt Brecht

PROFESSIONAL LEARNING COMMUNITIES

are schools that are characterized by shared purpose, collaborative activity, and collective responsibility among staff (Newmann & Wehlage, 1995). These schools respect learning, honor teaching, and teach for understanding (Darling-Hammond, 2001).

REACHING OUT TO THE KNOWLEDGE BASE

is an expression used to describe any process that brings new forms of knowledge and understanding into the school. Traditionally, the knowledge base and craft knowledge of teaching are transmitted through professional organizations, publications, and research. The knowledge base on teaching is now expanding to include a knowledge base on schooling practices and its impact upon learners and teachers.

SHARED DECISION MAKING

is an organizational practice that is grounded in the belief that all levels of the organization can and do influence the conditions and events in the environment. This means inviting interested people and all levels of the staff from principal to custodians to pool their resources to make informed decisions about what is best for the school.

SUBJECT MATTER NETWORKS

are groups of teachers organized around specific subject matter that seek to deepen teacher understanding of their content as well as their use of innovative teaching methodology.

VOLUNTARY FELLOWSHIP

is the willingness to join a group in pursuit of a common goal. In schools, this fellowship is grounded in a passion for learning and helping others.

...the bottom line is that teachers become school-based reformers only when they take on leadership for important parts of the school that lie beyond their classrooms.

—Roland Barth

WALK-THRU

Observe your school in action. Note indicators that provide evidence for the Professional Development of teachers. Select those indicators and create a Schoolwide Walk-Thru form so as to focus attention and to reinforce your school's accomplishments in this area.

This visual representation will help make your school's existing potential both public and visible. It will also create new energy needed to move to action.

SCHOOLWIDE WALK-THRU

- VISITING TEACHER
- ADMINISTRATOR
- OTHER _____

SCHOOL _____
_____
DATE _____

SIGNED _____

Supporting Professional Development

- Faculty Retreats/In-Service Projects
- Study Groups
- Collaborative Teaching Projects

Supporting Professional Development

- Teacher Mentors
- Affiliation With Local University
- Professional Affiliations

Supporting Professional Development

- Action Research Projects
- Professional Libraries
- Other

Figure 11.1

LOOKING WIDER

SUGGESTED READINGS

Barth, Roland S., "Learning by Heart," Jossey-Bass, 2001

Blankstein, Alan M., "Failure Is Not an Option," Corwin Press, 2004

Block, Peter, "The Answer to How Is Yes," Berrett-Koehler Publishers, Inc., 2002

Darling-Hammond, Linda, "The Right to Learn: A Blueprint for Creating Schools That Work," New Edition, Jossey-Bass, 2001

DuFour, Richard, and Eaker, Robert, "Professional Learning Communities at Work," National Educational Service and Association for Supervision and Curriculum Development, 1998

DuFour, Richard, Eaker, Robert, and DuFour, Rebecca, "On Common Ground," National Educational Service, 2005

Eaker, Robert, DuFour, Richard, and Burnette, Rebecca, "Getting Started," National Educational Service, 2002

Edman, Irwin (Introduction), "Essays by Ralph Waldo Emerson," Harper & Row, 1951

Newmann, Fred M., and Associates, "Authentic Achievement: Restructuring Schools for Intellectual Quality," Jossey-Bass, 1996

Sharratt, Lyn, and Fullan, Michael, "The School District That Did the Right Things Right," Journal of School Leadership, May 2006

Watts, Gary D., and Castle, Shari, "The Time Dilemma in School Restructuring," Phi Delta Kappan, December 1993

SIGNS OF SUCCESS WORTH FIGHTING FOR

- *An easily accessed professional development library*
- *Scheduled study groups and collaborative teacher inquiry projects*
- *Teacher retreats*
- *Time allocated for capacity building and testing innovative practices*
- *Published results of professional development initiatives*
- *Recognition for excellence in teaching*
- *Parent seminars to discuss the importance of the ongoing professional development of teachers*

LESSONS LEARNED

Example isn't another way to teach; it is the only way to teach.

——Albert Einstein

chapter one   LESSON 1:   In Learning Places, success is intentional.

chapter two   LESSON 2:   In Learning Places, the process of acquiring new knowledge and capacity is embedded more in the actual doing of the task and less in formal training.

chapter three   LESSON 3:   In Learning Places, individual student growth is the measure of choice when assessing learner performance.

chapter four   LESSON 4:   In Learning Places, promoting a sense of purpose and community is everybody's job.

chapter five   LESSON 5:   In Learning Places, making learning accessible throughout the school day and beyond is a major "gap closer."

chapter six   LESSON 6:   In Learning Places, professional rigor and a passion for teaching are contagious.

chapter seven   LESSON 7:   In Learning Places, effective teachers uncover material before they cover it.

chapter eight   LESSON 8:   In Learning Places, when subject matter is used to enliven thinking and create a larger context for knowing, experiencing, and understanding the world, more students get "turned on" to school.

chapter nine   LESSON 9:   In Learning Places, the symbiotic relationship between acquiring knowledge and using knowledge to deepen understanding is affirmed daily.

chapter ten   LESSON 10:   In Learning Places, knowledge is generative; it makes room for new growth.

chapter eleven   LESSON 11:   In Learning Places, the professional development of teachers is a means rather than an end.

CREATING A LEARNING PLACE

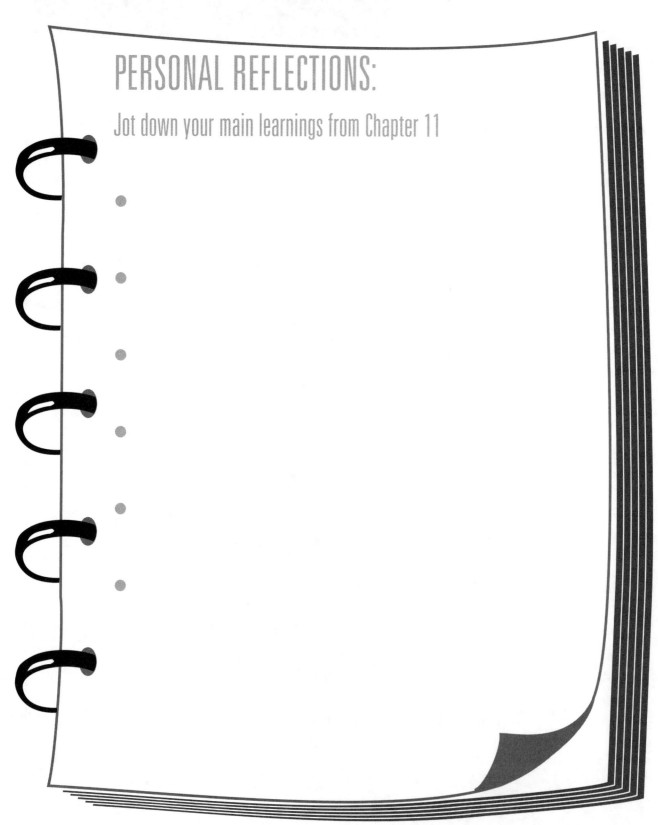

PERSONAL REFLECTIONS:

Jot down your main learnings from Chapter 11

CHAPTER TWELVE: REFRAMING SUCCESS

> *BIG IDEA — WHAT MAKES LIFE FUN AND WORK MEANINGFUL IS THE ACT OF RE-CREATION. A LEARNING PLACE IS WHERE TEACHERS, STUDENTS, AND PARENTS RE-CREATE.*

LESSON 12: ENERGY, NOT TIME, IS THE KEY TO SUSTAINABILITY.

If we combine the wisdom of the previous 11 chapters, they boil down to this: If we want to truly improve our schools, we need to create cultural change

a) by taking action, and

b) by acting differently—not only in our own context, but also in wider arenas.

Successful leaders are able to be simultaneously on the dance floor and the balcony.

—— Ronald A. Heifetz and Martin Linsky

Cultures get changed in a thousand small ways, not by dramatic announcements emanating from the board-room.

—— Peter Block

Recently, Fullan and his colleagues have been working on "Tri-Level Reform": what has to happen at the school/community level; the district level; and the state/policy level (Fullan, 2005; Fullan, Hill, and Crévola, 2006). We are after all talking about transforming the whole system. *Learning Places* says that the best way to change the system is to start at home, to strive to make one's own school and community a learning place of distinction. In this final chapter, we say be tuned in to the fact that you are engaged in a movement to change the whole system. This is not wishful thinking, but rather is engaging in action with this bigger purpose clearly in mind.

If the improvements you are making are going to have any staying power, the wider context within which you work must be part of the change. And to change the wider context you must participate in it. In our York Region example in Chapter 11, the principals and teachers are changing their context (i.e., the culture of the entire district) by engaging in it. They are interacting with other schools and with the district to help deepen their own school reform, as they change the context in which they work. They are explicitly aware that they are involved in a change far bigger than their own school. This is crucial if schools are to get any lasting breakthroughs.

Let us use an even larger example. The Province of Ontario in 2003 began tri-level reform across the whole system, starting with literacy and numeracy up to the age of 12 (grade 6), but now including high school reform. There are 72 (large) districts in Ontario with 4,000 elementary schools. The tri-level strategy involves mobilizing each of the three levels in partnership. It is very much a Learning Places writ large proposition.

If we take the literacy and numeracy goals, the strategy consists of focusing on instruction; negotiating jointly owned targets with all districts (who in turn do so with their schools); adding targeted resources for new leadership, instructional materials, and above all, capacity building (the latter involving new individual and collective knowledge, competencies, and commitments); using lateral capacity-building strategies to enable schools and districts to learn from each other; and using data to drive instruction—the latter occurs in two ways:

1) developing assessment for learning capacities as a high-yield strategy to influence specific instructional practice that addresses problems as they arise; and

2) creating a climate of positive pressure and transparent accountability. Negative pressure is when you compare all schools in a rank-ordered way, while positive pressure involves comparing schools facing similar situations with each other in order to learn about what makes for success and enable the learning to benefit all schools.

The Ontario strategy is very much based on the premise that it takes a system to raise all children, but such a system is not driven from the top; the strategy is based on the assumption that enabling, unlocking, responding to, stimulating, etc., the hearts and minds of those in all 4,000 schools will be necessary for any major breakthroughs. The strategy is already getting results. In the period 1999–2003 (before the initiation of the strategy), the literacy and numeracy results in the Province were flat lined or stagnant with little energy and no momentum. After six months of the new approach in 2004, Province–wide results in reading, writing, and mathematics for grade 6 students, for example, increased by 3 percentage points; in 2005, after 18 months these same results increased by a further 5%—the largest single-year increase since the provincial testing agency was established in 1997. And we are talking about 72 districts, 4,000 schools.

It is still too early to generalize or to indicate that the new movement is firmly established in Ontario. But we believe the message is clear: Schools work to create individual learning places 'in a thousand small ways." Look for and push for connections both inside and beyond your school and good things will happen within your school district and beyond. Learning places can show the way, and as their numbers increase they will attract more and more kindred spirits. Thus, breakthroughs will occur that will provide new possibilities never before thought possible. Learning Places are energizing, and if we get enough of them the system will become energized—and then we have a chance to sustain our work. Energy, not time, is the key to sustainability.

NOTE WELL:

While *Learning Places* is about changing your classroom, school, and community, it is really about transforming yourself as well as the whole system. Many practitioners changing local situations are really "System Thinkers in Action" (Fullan, 2005). Because they pursue moral purpose in a deep relentless way, and because to do this effectively they must enlarge their world of action with others inside and outside the school, system thinkers in action end up *changing context.* And when you change context, a whole new world is created.

Now that you have let these lessons massage your mind and heart so that you can "see" in a new way, do a Free Write in response to the following question: What am I going to do right now to use what I have learned about Learning Places to contribute to and learn from other schools in my district and elsewhere?

We shall not cease from exploration
And the end of all our exploring
Will be to arrive where we started
And know the place for the first time

— T.S. Eliot

A Free Write is your spontaneous or gut reaction to a key question. You should jot down, as quickly as you can, your gut stream of thought about the question.

What can I do right now to use what I have learned about Learning Places to contribute to and learn from similar schools in my district and elsewhere?

FREE WRITE

Learning Places is about creating a new world—not one created by someone else, but a place created for your students through your own actions. This is Moral Purpose with a powerful engine. Go for it!

Empowerment is embodied in the act of standing on our own ground, discovering our own voice, making our own choices. Regardless of the level of power and privilege we hold.

—— Peter Block

INDEX

**CORWIN
PRESS**

The Corwin Press logo—a raven striding across an open book—represents the union of courage and learning. Corwin Press is committed to improving education for all learners by publishing books and other professional development resources for those serving the field of PreK–12 education. By providing practical, hands-on materials, Corwin Press continues to carry out the promise of its motto: **"Helping Educators Do Their Work Better."**

The Ontario Principals' Council (OPC) is a voluntary professional association for principals and vice-principals in Ontario's public school system. We believe that exemplary leadership results in outstanding schools and improved student achievement. To this end, we foster quality leadership through world-class professional services and supports. As an ISO 9001 registered organization, we are committed to our statement that "quality leadership is our principal product."